W9-CUH-536

DISCOVER THE
BEST JOBS FOR YOU!

Books by Drs. Ron and Caryl Krannich

The Almanac of American Government Jobs and Careers
The Almanac of International Jobs and Careers
Best Jobs For the 1990s and Into the 21st Century
Careering and Re-Careering For the 1990s
The Complete Guide to International Jobs and Careers
The Complete Guide to Public Employment
Discover the Best Jobs For You!
Dynamite Answers to Interview Questions
Dynamite Cover Letters
Dynamite Resumes
Dynamite Tele-Search
The Educator's Guide to Alternative Jobs and Careers
Find a Federal Job Fast!
High Impact Resumes and Letters
Interview For Success
Job Search Letters That Get Results
Jobs For People Who Love Travel
Mayors and Managers
Moving Out of Education
Moving Out of Government
The New Network Your Way to Job and Career Success
The Politics of Family Planning Policy
Re-Careering in Turbulent Times
Salary Success
Shopping and Traveling in Exotic Asia
Shopping and Traveling in Exotic Hong Kong
Shopping and Traveling in Exotic India
Shopping and Traveling in Exotic Indonesia
Shopping and Traveling in Exotic Morocco
Shopping and Traveling in Exotic Singapore and Malaysia
Shopping and Traveling in Exotic Thailand
Shopping and Traveling the Exotic Philippines
Shopping in Exciting Australia and Papua New Guinea
Shopping in Exotic Places
Shopping the Exotic South Pacific

DISCOVER THE BEST JOBS FOR YOU!

Second Edition

Ronald L. Krannich, Ph.D.
Caryl Rae Krannich, Ph.D.

IMPACT PUBLICATIONS
Manassas Park, VA

DISCOVER THE BEST JOBS FOR YOU!

Second Edition

Copyright © 1993, 1991 by Ronald L. Krannich and Caryl Rae Krannich

All rights reserved. Printed in the United States of America. No part of this book may be used or reproduced in any manner whatsoever without written permission of the publisher: IMPACT PUBLICATIONS, 9201-N Manassas Drive, Manassas Park, VA 22111, Tel. 703/361-7300.

Library of Congress Cataloguing-in-Publication Data

Krannich, Ronald L.
  Discover the best jobs for you / Ronald L. Krannich, Caryl Rae Krannich.—2nd ed.
     p. cm.
  Rev. ed. of: Discover the right job for you! 1991.
  Includes bibliographical references and index.
  ISBN 0-942710-82-7: $24.95
  ISBN 0-942710-79-7 (pbk.): $11.95
  1. Job hunting. 2. Vocational interests. I. Krannich, Caryl Rae. II. Krannich, Ronald L. Discover the right job for you! III. Title.
HF53482.K69 1993
650.14—dc20

                92-39460
                    CIP

For information on distribution or quantity discount rates, Tel. 703/361-7300, FAX 703/335-9486, or write to: Sales Department, IMPACT PUBLICATIONS, 9104-N Manassas Dr., Manassas Park, VA 22111. Distributed to the trade by National Book Network, 4720 Boston Way, Suite A, Lanham, MD 20706, Tel. 301/459-8696.

CONTENTS

PREFACE

Millions of people each year find jobs and change careers. Some are more successful than others in finding the right job for them. For some, the process is relatively easy and results in rewarding jobs. For others, the process is painful and yields less than satisfactory results.

If you are looking for a job or contemplating a career change, this is a good time to take stock of your interests, values, abilities, skills, and goals **before** writing resumes, responding to job listings, or networking for job information. Unfortunately, many job seekers do last things first and thereby neglect to address the **basics** of the job finding process. This should not happen to you.

This book is all about doing first things first—assessing your interests, values, abilities, skills, stating your goals, and relating this information about yourself to specific jobs before going on to other job search steps that ultimately result in job interviews and offers. For the key to job search success lies in yourself—knowing who you are and what you want to do in reference to the world of work. You must answer important questions about yourself before you can communicate your qualifications and aspirations to employers.

We wrote this book because we saw a need to bring together some of the major thinking on self-assessment that would help guide job seekers through the job search maze. In so doing, we identify two different approaches that should assist you in clarifying what it is you do well, what you enjoy doing, and where you want to go. While each approach requires different investments of your time and energy as well as alternative ways of thinking about yourself, both approaches result in focusing your job search in directions that should please you. If followed properly, these approaches should put you on the road to finding the right job.

The following pages offer a combination of academic analysis and practical how-to advice. The academic side addresses several key issues central to the work of professional career counselors. Although this analysis has extremely important implications for nonprofessionals, many readers may wish to skip over this discussion, especially in Chapters Four and Fifteen. Most chapters address the practical how-tos of finding jobs and changing careers. They outline several options for discovering the best jobs for you.

We do not offer a new approach to finding jobs nor any magical formulas for success. Rather, we attempt to clarify the best approaches to finding jobs that begin with **you**. In so doing, we analyze and synthesize numerous approaches we feel offer you the best alternatives for finding your best jobs.

Our emphasis throughout this book is on **options**. There are alternative ways to reaching the same destination, but you first need a roadmap that identifies your options before you can decide which way to go. If, for example, you need to better understand your interests and skills and how they relate to different jobs, we outline alternative ways of doing so, from self-directed pencil and paper exercises to professionally administered tests and computer software programs. If you feel you need additional assistance, we identify numerous other books and services that can help you. As such, this book should serve as a useful resource for finding what you need in the process of discovering the best jobs for you. It should also help you better define your destination.

We wish to thank the many career counselors who contributed both directly and indirectly to this book. It is their on-the-ground work and enthusiasm to make a difference in the lives of others that ultimately brings clarity to this subject as well as demonstrates the effectiveness of the approaches outlined in the following chapters. We especially owe a debt of gratitude to William J. Banis who collaborated with Ron in previous books in identifying the many self-assessment approaches appearing in this book. His contributions are especially evident in the chapters on identifying skills and setting goals.

We wish you well in your search for the best jobs. But do us and yourself a favor: organize your thinking around doing first things first. Begin your job search by first examining who you are and where you want to go. Then take action based upon a clear objective. As you will discover in the following pages, **the single-minded pursuit of an objective** may be your greatest asset, regardless of the method you use to define your objective. Objectives do make a significant difference.

Whatever you do, get organized for what may become the greatest adventure of your life—discovering the best jobs for you!

Ron and Caryl Krannich

Chapter One

DO FIRST THINGS FIRST

Many people simply love their work. Indeed, they believe they have the best job in the world. They find their work challenging, satisfying, and fun. They are rewarded in many ways, from the interesting nature of their work to the talented people they work with. They receive good pay and benefits. And their career future looks bright. They are the fortunate ones.

How do people find their best jobs? What is it they do that others don't? Are they more intelligent than others? Do they have extraordinary education, training, and experience? Perhaps they know the right people. Or maybe their timing is right, or they are just lucky.

The best jobs go to those who know who they are, what they want, and where they are going. They have clear goals, keep focused on those goals, and make intelligent moves within the job market. They understand themselves, the job market, and employers. They know how to identify the right employers as well as how to best communicate their qualifications to employers. Most important of all, they know which jobs are best for them.

GET READY FOR YOUR FUTURE

Most adults spend between 35 and 60 hours a week in work related activities. Some greet the Monday morning alarm clock with excitement and anticipation. Others dread the start of a new work week. Which are you or which will you become?

What do you want to do next month, next year, or even the rest of your life? Do you want a job that leads to major career advancement, more money, and greater power, or do you prefer less responsibility, less stress, and a slower pace? Perhaps you are primarily interested in pursuing a particular lifestyle centered around skills you most enjoy using? Do you want to work for someone else or run your own show? Where do you see your career and lifestyle 5, 10, or 20 years from now?

These questions lie at the heart of discovering the best job for you. They are the subject of this book. More important, they should become your central concerns as you develop a well organized and coherent plan for job success.

FIND THE BEST JOBS

Many people end up in the wrong jobs, because they fail to plan their careers around their major strengths and motivations. Not knowing what they do well and enjoy doing, they primarily seek jobs they think might be good for them in terms of salary and benefits. They seldom view jobs as being right for them. They fail to relate jobs to their long-term patterns of interests, skills, and abilities. Once on the job, they may discover the job is an inappropriate "fit" for their abilities and motivational patterns. Salary and benefits become secondary considerations as they find few on-the-job rewards.

Few people are lucky enough to find jobs and pursue careers they really love. This is not to say most people are unhappy with their present jobs. Contrary to what many writers tell us—that nearly 80 percent of the workforce is unhappy with their jobs—annual national surveys continue to confirm that nearly 80 percent of today's workforce is relatively content with their present jobs. But could many of these people do much better if they used a different approach to finding jobs and advancing their careers?

Concerned with either keeping their present jobs or just finding one to pay the bills, most people seldom focus on the larger question of what jobs are really right for them. Instead, when looking for employment, they look **outside** themselves by focusing on "where the jobs are." This approach leads them on a search for job vacancy announcements that look interesting to them rather than for jobs that may be right for them. They become preoccupied with fitting into the requirements of different jobs rather than trying to find jobs that are fit for them.

> *The secret to discovering the best jobs for you is much more than an external search for "where the jobs are."*

The secret to discovering the best jobs for you is much more than an external search for "where the jobs are." It goes beyond the major initial approach of job seekers—to quickly put together a resume so they can respond to vacancy announcements. While finding vacancy announcements and writing resumes are important elements in a job search, they should not be the first steps. They are not even the second or third things you need to do. They are intermediate activities that lie closer to the end of a job search.

At the very minimum, finding the best jobs for you begins with **you**—knowing your interests, values, abilities, skills, motivations, and dreams. You must analyze, synthesize, and reformulate this self-assessment information into a powerful objective. This objective, in turn, provides the foundation for a well organized job search that will ultimately link your strengths and goals to the needs of employers.

Your first task should be to get to know yourself better in terms of where you have been going in the past, where you are at present, and where you wish to go in the future. By initially focusing on your interests, skills, and abilities—rather than alternative job vacancies you feel you might be able to fit into—you begin building a sound basis for giving yourself positive career direction for many years to come.

This book is all about doing first things first. And the first thing you want to do is to answer the most important questions relating to your interests, values, abilities, skills, and objectives. In other words, you need to identify what it is you do well and enjoy doing **prior to** identifying where the jobs are and how to get one. The pages that follow show you how to best do this as you put yourself on a sound road to long-term career success.

DISCOVER A JOB FIT FOR YOU

Our major concern is that you find a job that is fit for you rather than one you think you might be able to fit into. This is an important distinction central to the remaining chapters in this book. Trying to "fit into a job" is the typical way most people find and keep jobs. They look for job vacancies and then try to stress those qualifications that will help them get the job. While some people find jobs they enjoy by using this approach, others are less fortunate. They often discover they are in the wrong job.

On the other hand, finding a job "fit for you" is what this book is all about. Our approach is based on a great deal of experience and common sense regarding how to best find and keep a job as well as advance a career. Time and again job seekers discover it is more important to know what they want to do than to know where the job vacancies can be found. It's essential to know what you do well (abilities and skills), what you enjoy doing (interests and values), and what you want to do (objective) before writing each section of your resume or going for a job interview. If you do these first things first, you are more likely to find a job fit for you rather than one you may or may not fit into well.

GET ORGANIZED FOR SUCCESS

This book is all about doing first things first—assessing your interests, abilities, and skills and formulating these into a powerful objective that will link you to the right job. This is not a book on "what the jobs are" or "where the jobs are" or even "how to get a job." You will find numerous such books available today that primarily list alternative jobs and careers. Some of the best such books are identified in our bibliography (Chapter Fifteen) and in the order form at the end of this book. A few books attempt to identify the 100+ "hottest" jobs and careers for the 1990s. Others are primarily directories of the most widely available jobs today. And still others attempt to show readers how to get into a few of today's best paying jobs.

We focus on the important **linkage** between you and alternative jobs. Our approach begins and ends with you in reference to the job market. While you eventually need to research alternative jobs and careers (Chapter Twelve) as well as survey job vacancies, you first need to do what we outline in the first eleven chapters—discover what you do well and enjoy doing and what you want to do in the years ahead. Armed with this self knowledge, you will be in the best position to know what particular jobs and careers you should pursue. You will know that while some jobs may look interesting, they are inappropriate for your particular mix of interests and abilities. You will save a great deal of time and effort, avoid future disappointments, and enjoy what you will be doing in the future if you read this book prior to going on to finding a specific job you think might be good for you.

> *Armed with this self knowledge, you will be in the best position to know what particular jobs and careers you should pursue.*

The chapters that follow are designed to easily walk you through the process of self-discovery. After examining alternative jobs and careers in Chapter Two and your job search and skills needs in Chapter Three, we examine different approaches to finding a job in Chapter Four. We conclude with advice on organizing a job search around the notion of doing "first things first" in the process of achieving job search success. Chapter Four is the critical overview chapter that shows you how all the job search pieces fit together as you face the task of organizing each step of your job search.

The remaining chapters take you step-by-step through the process of identifying your pattern of interests, values, abilities, skills, and motivations and then formulating them into a powerful job objective that will give your job search the necessary direction for success. Central to these chapters are two very different approaches to self-assessment and career direction.

DETERMINISTIC/ PREDESTINATION APPROACH

The first approach is widely practiced by a particular group of career counselors who believe in the power of predestination, the magic of testing, and the predictive power of probability. This approach is represented in its most extreme form by Richard Bolles (*What Color Is Your Parachute?*, *Three Boxes of Life*, and *The New Quick Job Hunting Map*) and Arthur Miller and Ralph Mattson (*The Truth About You*) and espoused by a legion of career counselors raised on the unquestioned and somewhat naive approach of these writers/practitioners. Basic to this approach is both a deterministic and probabilistic theory of individual behavior—your future performance will most likely be a repeat performance of your past patterns of behavior. Major proponents justify using this approach on explicit and somewhat controversial religious grounds: since God has put his imprint on you and you cannot escape your fate, you need to discover what he has pre-ordained for you. The approach ostensibly uncovers God's vision for you in the form of a "career map."

This deterministic/predestination approach takes you down a narrow and somewhat pessimistic road where you are advised to be "realistic" about your future. An analysis of historical data on you—rather than information on your future aspirations—should determine where you will go in the future. By discovering your past patterns of motivated abilities and skills, you will be able to formulate realistic career goals as well as an appropriate job search action plan.

Despite claims of effectiveness, doses of religious fundamentalism, and some hocus-pocus, most self-assessment devices using this deterministic/predestination approach are designed to reconstruct your past "patterns" of work behavior. We identify many of the most popular such devices and assess both their strengths and weaknesses.

SELF-TRANSFORMATION APPROACH

The second approach is widely used in business—primarily sales and entrepreneurship—and in some religious circles. This is a self-help psychological approach centered around such notions as "self-transformation," "thinking big," "following your dreams," "positive thinking," "you can be anything you want to be," and "reach for the stars." It's the basic motivational approach used in such direct-sales operations as Amway, Shaklee, and Tupperware as well as in real estate and insurance; the popular wealth building approaches based on the self-motivational philosophies of Napolean Hill (*Think and Grow Rich*), Maltz Maxwell (*Psycho-Cybernetics*), David Schwartz (*The Magic of Thinking Big*), Claude Bristol (*The Magic of Believing*), Anthony Robbins (*Personal Power*), Zig Ziglar (*How to Get What You Want*), Og Mandino (*Secrets of Success*) and many others; and the secular-religious writings of Dr. Robert H. Schuller (*You Can Become the Person You Want to Be*), Dr. Norman Vincent Peale (*The Power of Positive Thinking*), and Rabbi Harold Kushner (*When All You've Ever Wanted Isn't Enough*). Practitioners of this approach do not dwell on history. Indeed, one's history and past patterns of behavior are often seen as the **problem** rather the solution for charting a new future. These self-help philosophers see the past as an impediment—something people need to break away from as they transform themselves and head in new directions. Being "realistic" is not a major concern, because realism is most likely a function of one's past patterns of behavior which are blinders to the future. These approaches stress the importance of setting high level—even unrealistic—goals and then developing the power to stay highly motivated and focused on those goals. Being single-mindedly focused in pursuing big goals is the basis for breaking out of past patterns as individuals embark on a new and hopefully brighter future.

At first glance these are radically different approaches that can produce very different outcomes for you. The first approach used by most career counselors is conservative, deterministic, probabilistic, and realistic. The second approach is radical, risky, and refreshing. Both face a fundamental dilemma when dealing with the future:

How can you chart your future if it is merely a
reflection of your past, or if it is based on a
great deal of unrealistic big thinking?

The chapters that follow show how both approaches can best work for you. Each has certain strengths and weaknesses, and each works well for different people, depending on how they wish to chart their future. For some, the deterministic/predestination approach provides an excellent map for clarifying goals and organizing a well-focused job search centering around one's major strengths. For others, who are interested in making major changes in their behavior, this approach is too limiting. We outline how they can best make changes without becoming captives of their pasts or frustrated by an inability to attain their aspirations.

WHERE DO YOU GO FROM HERE?

We wish you well as you take this journey into the wild and sometimes confusing world of self-discovery. While we are primarily concerned at this stage in taking you through the most critical initial stages of a job search, we also recognize the need to continue on through other important stages that result in meeting potential employers and receiving job offers. These other steps are outlined in our other books: *Careering and Re-Careering For the 1990s, High Impact Resumes and Letters, Dynamite Resumes, Dynamite Cover Letters, Job Search Letters That Get Results, Dynamite Answers to Interview Questions, Interview For Success, Dynamite Tele-Search, The New Network Your Way to Job and Career Success,* and *Salary Success.* We also address particular job and career fields in the following books: *The Best Jobs For the 1990s and Into the 21st Century, The Complete Guide to Public Employment, Find a Federal Job Fast, The Complete Guide to International Jobs and Careers, The Almanac of American Government Jobs and Careers, The Almanac of International Jobs and Careers, Jobs For People Who Love Travel,* and *The Educator's Guide to Alternative Jobs and Careers.* These and many other job search books are outlined in the final chapter of this book. They are available in many bookstores and libraries. For your convenience, they also can be ordered directly from Impact Publications by completing the order form at the end of this book or by acquiring a copy of the publisher's catalog.

Contact Impact Publications to receive a free copy of the most comprehensive career catalog available today—*"Jobs and Careers for the 1990s."* For the latest edition of this catalog of over 1,400 annotated job and career resources, complete the order form on page 214 or write to:

IMPACT PUBLICATIONS
ATTN: Free Catalog
9104-N Manassas Drive
Manassas Park, VA 22111

They will send you a copy upon request. This 48-page annotated catalog contains almost every important career and job finding resource available today, including many titles that are difficult if not impossible to find in bookstores and libraries. You will find everything from additional self-assessment books to books on resume writing, interviewing, government and international jobs, military, women, minorities, students, entrepreneurs as well as videos and computer software programs. This is an excellent resource for keeping in touch with the major resources that can assist you with every stage of your job search as well as with your future career development plans.

DISCOVER THE BEST JOBS FOR YOU

The following pages are designed to assist you in developing an effective job search that will lead to discovering the best jobs for you. It addresses the **fundamentals** for getting yourself organized and focused on what it is you need to do to get that job. If you follow our advice, do first things first, and implement with persistence, you can join thousands of others who have learned the secrets to discovering their best jobs today and in the decade ahead!

Chapter Two

THE BEST JOBS
FOR TOMORROW

The best jobs for you hopefully will also be amongst the 100 best jobs predicted for the 1990s and into the 21st century. These are some of the fastest growing jobs that will generate a large number of job opportunities. Many of these jobs also offer excellent salaries and opportunities for advancement. They will be some of the most sought-after jobs in the decade ahead.

Let's examine what the futurists identify as some of the best jobs and careers in the decade ahead before we turn to you, the individual, who needs to identify what is really best for you.

This chapter should in no way imply that the best jobs for you will be found amongst the so-called "hot" jobs for the 1990s. Indeed, the best jobs for you will most likely be discovered by thoroughly understanding your interests, skills, and abilities rather than through some "objective" assessment of "where the jobs are."

WHAT ARE THE JOBS?

"**Where** are the jobs, and **how** do I get one?" These are the first two questions most people ask when seeking employment. But one other equally important question should precede these traditional questions:

"**What** are the jobs of tomorrow?"

For the nature of jobs is changing rapidly in response to (1) techno-logical innovations, (2) the development and application of new technology to the work place, and (3) the demand for a greater variety of consumer services. Today's job seeker needs answers to the "what," "where," and "how" of jobs for the 1990s and beyond.

Many jobs in the year 2000 will look very different from those in the 1980s. Indeed, if we project present trends into the future and believe what futurists tell us about emerging new careers, the 21st century will offer unprecedented and exciting careering and re-careering opportunities.

But such changes and opportunities have costs. The change in jobs and occupations will be so rapid that skills learned today may become obsolete in another five to ten years. Therefore, knowing what the jobs are becomes a prerequisite to knowing how to prepare for them, find them, and change them in the future.

If you wish to identify a growing career field to plan your own career, do so only after you identify your interests, skills, and abilities.

BEWARE OF CHANGING OCCUPATIONAL PROFILES

A few words of caution are in order on how you should and should not use the information in this chapter. If you wish to identify a growing career field to plan your own career, do so only after you identify your interests, skills, and abilities. The next step is to acquire the training before conducting a job search. Only then should you seriously consider pursuing what appears to be a growing field.

At the same time, you should be aware that the statistics and projections on growing industrial and occupational fields may be inaccurate. First, they are based on traditional models and economic studies conducted by the U.S. Department of Labor, Bureau of Labor Statistics. Unlike fortune tellers and soothsayers who communicate in another world and many futurists who engage in "informed flights of fancy" and "brainstorming," the Bureau conducts "empirical studies" which assume a steady rate of economic growth throughout the 1990s—similar to the 1950s. Such occupational projections are nothing more than "best guesses" based upon a traditional model which assumes continual, linear growth. This planning model does not deal well with the reality of cyclical changes, as evidenced by its failures during the turbulent 1980s when boom and bust cycles, coupled with the emergence of unique events and crises, invalidated many of the Bureau's employment and occupational forecasts. For example, the Department of Labor projected a high unemployment rate of 7.6 percent for 1982; but in 1982 unemployment stood at 10.8 percent. In addition, the deepening recession and the government program cuts brought on by a series of international crises, domestic economic failures, and ideological changes were unanticipated developments which resulted in the actual decline in public employment for the first time since World War II. Thus, in 1982 there were 316,000 fewer public employees than in the year before! The turbulent 1990s may well provide us with more unique economic scenarios which produce similar unpredictable outcomes.

Second, during a period of turbulent change, occupational profiles may become quickly outdated. Training requirements change, and thus individuals encounter greater uncertainty in career choices. For example, based on trend analyses, many people believe that promising careers lie ahead for computer programmers. This may be true if thousands of newly trained individuals do not glut the job market with computer programming skills. Moreover, it may be true if computer technology remains stagnant and the coming generation of self-programmed computers does not make computer programmers—like their keypunch counterparts in the 1960s and 1970s—obsolete. If either, let alone both, of these "if's" occur, many computer programming jobs may disappear, and many newly trained computer programmers may become displaced workers in need of re-careering.

A similar situation arises for students pursuing the much glamorized MBA and law degrees. Today, as more MBA's graduate and glut the job market with questionable skills, the glitter surrounding this degree has diminished; the MBA may fast become an obsolete degree as employers turn to degree fields that emphasize greater communication, analytical, and technical skills.

A similar situation appears relevant to the law field. While the demand for lawyers increased substantially in the 1980s, and a large number of students continue to enroll in law schools, competition for legal positions may be keen in the years ahead as more and more law graduates flood a shrinking job market. Contrary to most future job growth projections for lawyers, opportunities for lawyers may not increase much during the 1990s. The demand for lawyers may actually decline due to substantial restructuring of the legal profession as lawyers become more competitive, promote more efficient legal services, hire more paralegals, change fee and billing practices, introduce more technology to traditional legal tasks, and develop more do-it-yourself legal approaches; as the criminal justice system undergoes restructuring; and as Americans become less litigious due to the high costs of pursuing legal action.

EXPECT JOB GROWTH IN MOST OCCUPATIONS AND FOR MOST GROUPS

The growth in jobs has been steady during the past three to four decades. From 1955 to 1980, for example, the number of jobs increased from 68.7 to 105.6 million. This represented an average annual increase of about 1.5 million new jobs. During the 1970s the number of jobs increased by over 2 million per year. And between the years 1983 and 1988 the number of jobs increased by 16 million, a phenomenal annual growth rate of nearly 3 million!

Job growth during the 1990s is expected to slow but remain steady at about 1.5 million new jobs each year, reflecting the coming demographic changes in society. By the year 2005 the labor force should consist of nearly 151 million workers—up 21 percent from 1990.

Highlighting these patterns of job growth are 15 forecasts, based on U.S. Department of Labor data and projections, which represent the confluence of demographic, economic, and technological changes in society during the 1990s:

EMPLOYMENT FORECASTS FOR THE 1990s

1. **Growth of the labor force slows during the 1990s.**

   The growth in the labor force will slow to 151 million by
   the year 2005—a 21 percent increase over the 1990 level.
   This represents half the rate of increase during the previous 15-year period, and it reflects the overall slow growth
   of the population, with a less than zero population birth
   rate of 0.7 percent per year.

2. **Labor force will become even more racially and ethni-
   cally diverse than in previous decades.**

   The racial and ethnic mix of the work force in the year
   2005 will be even more diverse than in the year 1990
   given the differential birth and immigration rates of
   various racial and ethnic groups. Blacks, Hispanics,
   Asians, and other minority groups will represent 27
   percent of the work force—up from 22 percent in 1990.
   These groups also will account for 35 percent of labor
   force entrants between 1990 and 2005.

3. **Fewer young people will enter the job market.**

   The number of 16 to 24 year-olds entering the job market
   declined between 1975 and 1990 by 1.4 million or 6
   percent. Their numbers will increase by 2.8 million during
   1990-2005, reflecting an 13 percent increase. These new
   entrants represent the children of the baby-boom generation who began entering the job market after 1992. The
   number of 22 to 24 year-olds entering the job market will
   continue to decline until 1998. The youth share of the
   labor force will fall to 16 percent by 2005. This represents
   a significant decline—down from 23 percent in 1972, 20
   percent in 1987, and 17 percent in 1990. Businesses
   depending on this age group for students, recruits,
   customers, and part-time workers—especially colleges, the
   Armed Forces, eating and drinking establishments, and
   retail stores—must draw from a smaller pool of young

people. Competition among young people for entry-level jobs will decline accordingly.

4. The work force will continue to gray as it becomes older and older.

As the baby-boom generation of the 1960s and 1970s becomes more middle-aged, the number of 25 to 54 year olds in the labor force will increase substantially by the year 2000—with 72 percent or nearly 3 of every 4 workers, being between the ages of 25 and 54. This represents a significant increase from 40 percent in 1988 and 36 percent in 1976. Between 1990 and 2005 the number of older workers, aged 55 years and above, will grow twice as fast as the labor force as a whole.

5. Women will enter the labor force in growing numbers.

Women will represent over half of all entrants into the labor force during the 1990s. While accounting for 39 percent of the labor force in 1972 and 41 percent of the labor force in 1976, women in the year 2005 will constitute over 47 percent of the labor force. By the year 2005, 4 out of 5 women between the ages of 25 and 54 will be in the labor force.

6. Education requirements for most new jobs will continue to rise.

Most new jobs will require strong basic education skills, such as reading, writing, oral communication, and computation. Many of these jobs will include important high-tech components which will require previous specialized education and training as well as the demonstrated ability to learn and acquire nontraditional education and training to continuously re-tool skills.

7. The fastest growing occupations will be in executive, managerial, professional, and technical fields—all requiring the highest levels of education and skill.

Three-quarters of the fastest growing occupational groups will be executive, administrative, and managerial; professional specialty; and technicians and related support occupations—occupations that require the highest levels of education and skill. Few opportunities will be available for high school dropouts or those who cannot read or follow directions. A combination of greater emphasis on productivity in the work place, increased automation, technological advances, innovations, changes in consumer demands, and import substitutions will decrease the need for workers with little formal education and few skills—helpers, laborers, assemblers, and machine operators.

8. **Employment will increase for most occupations in the 1990s.**

As the population continues to grow and become more middle-aged and affluent, demands for more services will increase accordingly. Except in the cases of agriculture, mining, and traditional manufacturing, the 1990s will be a period of steady to significant job growth in all occupations. Over 25 million jobs will be added to the U.S. economy between the years 1990 and 2005. However, new jobs will be unevenly distributed across major industrial and occupational groups due to the restructuring of the economy and the increased education and training requirements for most jobs.

9. **The greatest growth in jobs will take place in service industries and occupations.**

Over 90 percent of all new jobs in the 1990s will be in the service-producing industries with services such as legal, business (advertising, accounting, word processing, and computer support), and healthcare leading the way. The number of jobs in services is expected to rise by 35 percent between 1990 and 2005, from 38 to 50.5 million. Health and business will be the fastest growing service industries during this period. Social, legal, and engineering and management services industries will also exhibit strong growth.

10. **Retail trade will be the second fastest growing industrial sector in the 1990s.**

   Employment in the retail trade is expected to increase by 26 percent, from 19.7 to 24.8 million during the 1990 to 2005 period.

11. **Government employment will increase at different rates for different levels of government as well as for governmental units in different regions of the country.**

   Federal government employment will remain relatively level, increasing by less than 1.0 percent each year as the federal government continues on a long-term trend to contract-out government services rather than increase in-house personnel. Except during recessionary periods, state and local government employment will increase by 2 to 3 percent each year with local governments in the rapidly developing and relatively affluent cities and counties of the West and Southwest experiencing the largest employment growth rates. State and local government employment is likely to decline in many areas of the Northeast. Excluding public education and public hospitals, for the period 1990 to 2005 government employment is expected to increase by 14 percent, from 9.5 million to 10.8 million jobs.

12. **Employment growth in education at all levels will be incremental.**

   Both public and private education is expected to add 2.3 million jobs to the 9.4 million employed in 1990. Employment in education will increase slightly at all levels due to projected population and enrollment increases. Between 1990 and 2005, elementary school age population should rise by 3.8 million, secondary by 3.2 million, and postsecondary by 1.4 million. Accordingly, job opportunities should increase for teachers, teacher aides, counselors, and administrative staff.

13. Jobs in manufacturing will decline throughout the 1990s.

Manufacturing jobs are expected to decline by 3 percent, from the 1990 level of 19.1 million. Most of the decline will affect production jobs; professional and technical positions in manufacturing will increase. These declines will be due to productivity gains achieved through automation and improved management as well as the closing of less efficient plants.

14. Employment in agriculture, forestry, fishing, and mining jobs will continue to decline.

Employment in agriculture, forestry, and fishing is expected to decline by 6 percent, from 3.3 to 3.1 million, reflecting a decrease of nearly 410,000 self-employed workers. Wage and salary positions in agricultural, forestry, and fishing services will increase by 214,000. Strong growth will take place in agricultural services industry, especially landscape, horticultural, and farm management services. Much of the self-employment decline in agriculture will be due to the closing of lucrative export markets as the productivity of agriculture abroad improves and new hybrid crops are introduced from genetic engineering breakthroughs to solve many of the world's food problems. Employment in mining is expected to decline by 6 percent—from 712,000 to 669,000. These figures assume that domestic oil production will drop and oil imports will rise sharply.

15. Glamorous new occupations, responding to new technological developments and consumer demands, will offer exciting new careering and re-careering opportunities for future job seekers who are well educated and skilled in the jobs of tomorrow.

New occupations, created through a combination of technological innovations and new service demands, will provide excellent career opportunities for those who possess the necessary skills and drive to succeed in the 1990s. New occupations with such names as bionic-electronic technician, holographic inspector, cryonics technician, and aquaculturist will enter our occupational vocabulary during the 1990s.

PROJECT OCCUPATIONAL PROFILES THROUGH THE YEAR 2005

The U.S. Department of Labor divides the economy into two types of industries and nine industrial sectors for projecting employment trends:

1. Services-producing industries

- Services
- Retail and wholesale trade
- Finance, insurance, and real estate
- Transportation, communications, and public utilities
- Government

2. Goods-producing industries

- Construction
- Manufacturing
- Mining
- Agriculture, forestry, and fishing

Throughout the 1990s most job growth will take place among service-producing industries. Assuming the latter half of the 1990s will be a decade of rising incomes and living standards, individuals will place greater demand on health care, entertainment, and business and financial services. With the continuing growth of cities, suburbs and exurbans, the demand for local government services should increase.

The second largest service-producing industry generating jobs in the 1990s will be wholesale and retail trade. Again, if we assume incomes and living standards will rise throughout the 1990s, the largest number of new jobs in the trade sector will be found among eating and drinking establishments. Other retail trade firms that should generate large numbers of new jobs will be department stores, grocery stores, and new car dealerships. The largest contributors to new jobs in the wholesale trade will be firms handling machinery, electric goods, and motor vehicles.

Between 1990 and 2005 the Department of Labor anticipates the following occupational growth and decline patterns for service and goods producing industries:

TOMORROW'S JOBS BY INDUSTRIAL SECTOR

Industrial Profile: The long-term shift from goods-producing to service-producing employment is expected to continue. For example, service-producing industries—including transportation, communications, and utilities; retail and wholesale trade; services; government; and finance, insurance, and real estate—are expected to account for approximately 23 million of the 24.6 million new jobs created by the year 2005. In addition, the services division within this sector—which includes health, business, and educational services—contains 16 of the 20 fastest growing industries, and 12 of the 20 industries adding the most jobs. Expansion of service sector employment is linked to a number of factors, including changes in consumer tastes and preferences, legal and regulatory changes, advances in science and technology, and changes in the way businesses are organized and managed.

Service-Producing Industries

1. Services: Services is both the largest and the fastest growing division within the service-producing sector. This division provided 38 million jobs in 1990; employment is expected to rise 34.7 percent to 50.5 million by 2005, accounting for almost one-half of all new jobs. Jobs will be found in small firms and in large corporations, in State and local government, and in industries as diverse as banking, hospitals, data processing, and management consulting. The two largest industry groups in this division, health services and business services, are projected to continue to grow very fast. In addition, social, legal, and engineering and management services industries further illustrate this division's strong growth.

Health care will continue to be one of the fastest growing industries in the economy. Employment in the health services industries is projected to grow from 8.9 to 12.8 million. Improvements in medical technology, and a growing and aging population will increase the demand for health services. Employment in home health care services—the fastest growing industry in the economy—nursing homes, and offices and clinics of physicians and other health practitioners is projected to increase the most rapidly throughout this period. However, not all health industries will grow at the same rapid rate. For example, hospitals, both public and private, will continue to be the largest, but slowest growing health care industry.

Business services industries also will generate many jobs. Employment is expected to grow from 5.2 million in 1990 to 7.6 million in 2005. Personnel supply services, made up primarily of temporary help agencies, is the largest sector in this group and will continue to add many jobs. However, due to the slowdown in labor force participation by young women, and the proliferation of personnel supply firms in recent years, this industry will grow more slowly than during the 1975-90 period, although still faster than the average for all industries. Business services also includes one of the fastest growing industries in the economy—computer and data processing services. This industry's rapid growth stems from advances in technology, world wide trends toward office and factory automation, and increases in demand from business firms, government agencies, and individuals.

Education, both private and public, is expected to add 2.3 million jobs to the 9.4 million in 1990. This increase reflects population growth and, in turn, rising enrollments projected for elementary, secondary, and postsecondary schools. The elementary school age population (ages 5-13) will rise by 3.8 million between 1990 and 2005, the secondary school age (14-17) by 3.2 million, and the traditional postsecondary school age (18-24) by 1.4 million. In addition, continued rising enrollments of older, foreign, and part-time students are expected to enhance employment in postsecondary education. Not all of the increase in employment in education, however, will be for teachers; teacher aides, counselors, and administration staff also are projected to increase.

Employment in social services is expected to increase by 1.1 million, bringing the total to 2.9 million by 2005, reflecting the growing elderly population. For example, residential care institutions, which provide around-the-clock assistance to older persons and others who have limited ability for self-care, is projected to be one of the fastest growing industries in the U.S. economy. Other social services industries that are projected to grow rapidly include child daycare services and individual and miscellaneous social services, which includes elderly daycare and family social services.

2. Retail and wholesale trade: Employment in retail and wholesale trade is expected to rise by 26 and 16 percent, respectively; from 19.7 to 24.98 million in retail trade and from 6.2 to 7.2 million in wholesale trade. Guided by higher levels of personal income and continued increases in women's labor force participation, the fastest projected job growth in retail trade is in apparel and accessory stores and eating and drinking establishments, with the latter employing the most workers in this sector. Substantial numerical increases in retail employment are anticipated in food stores, automotive dealers and service stations, and general merchandise stores.

3. Finance, insurance, and real estate: Employment is expected to increase by 21 percent—adding 1.4 million jobs to the 1990 level of 6.7 million. The demand for financial products and services is expected to continue unabated, but bank mergers, consolidations, and closings—resulting from overexpansion and competition from nonbank corporations that offer bank-like services—are expected to limit job growth. The fastest growing industry within this sector is expected to be nondepository holding and investment offices, which includes businesses that compete with banks, such as finance companies and mortgage brokers.

4. Transportation, communications, and public utilities: Overall employment will increase by 15 percent. Employment in the transportation sector is expected to increase by 25 percent, from 3.6 to 4.4 million jobs. Truck transportation will account for 47 percent of all new jobs; air transportation will account for 32 percent. The projected gains in transportation jobs reflect the continued shift from rail to road freight transportation, rising personal incomes, and growth in foreign trade. In addition, deregulation in the transportation industry has increased personal and business travel options, spurring strong job growth in the passenger transportation arrangement industry, which includes travel agencies. Reflecting laborsaving technology and industry competition, employment in communications is projected to decline by 13 percent. Employment in utilities, however, is expected to grow about as fast as the average, adding 160,000 new jobs, highlighted by one of the fastest growing industries in the economy—water supply and sanitary services.

5. Government: Between 1990 and 2005, government employment, excluding public education and public hospitals, is expected to increase 14 percent, from 9.5 million to 10.8 million jobs. This growth will occur in State and local government; employment in the Federal Government is expected to decline by 31,000 jobs.

Goods-Producing Industries

Employment in this sector peaked in the late 1970's, and has not recovered from the recessionary period of the early 1980's and the trade imbalances that began in the mid-1980's. Although overall employment in goods-producing industries is expected to show little change, growth prospects within the sector vary considerably.

1. Construction: Construction, the only goods-producing industry projected to grow, is expected to add 923,000 jobs between 1990 and 2005. Construction employment is expected to increase by 18 percent, from 5.1 to 6.1 million. Increases in road and bridge construction will offset the slowdown in demand for new housing, reflecting the slowdown in population growth and the overexpansion of office building construction in recent years.

2. Manufacturing: Manufacturing employment is expected to decline by 3 percent from the 1990 level of 19.1 million. The projected loss of manufacturing jobs reflects productivity gains achieved from increased investment in manufacturing technologies as well as a winnowing out of less efficient operations.

The composition of manufacturing employment is expected to shift since most of the jobs that will disappear are production jobs. The number of professional, technical, and managerial positions in manufacturing firms will increase.

3. Mining: Mining employment is expected to decline from 712,000 to 669,000—a 6-percent decline. Underlying this projection is the assumption that domestic oil production will drop and oil imports will rise sharply, reducing the employment in the crude petroleum industry. However, the expected rise in oil prices should spark exploration and, consequently, a slight increase in employment in the oil field services industry. In addition, employment in coal mining should continue to decline sharply due to the expanded use of laborsaving machinery.

4. Agriculture, forestry, and fishing: Overall employment in agriculture, forestry, and fishing has been declining for many decades and this trend is expected to continue—the number of jobs is projected to decline by 6 percent, from 3.3 million to 3.1 million.

The decline in agricultural, forestry, and fishing jobs reflects a decrease of 410,000 in the number of self-employed workers. Wage and salary positions are expected to increase by 214,000—with especially strong growth in the agricultural services industry, which includes landscape, horticultural, and farm management services.

EXAMINE GROWING AND DECLINING OCCUPATIONS

The Department of Labor divides occupations into 16 broad groups based on the Standard Occupational Classification, the classification system used by all government agencies for collecting occupational employment information:

- Executive, administrative, and managerial occupations
- Engineers, scientists, and related occupations
- Social science, social service, and related occupations
- Teachers, librarians, and counselors
- Health-related occupations
- Writers, artists, and entertainers
- Technologists and technicians
- Marketing and sales occupations
- Administrative support occupations, including clerical
- Service occupations
- Agricultural and forestry occupations
- Mechanics and repairers
- Construction occupations

- Production occupations
- Transportation and material moving occupations
- Handlers, equipment cleaners, helpers, and laborers

Assuming a moderate rate of economic growth throughout the 1990s—not boom and bust cycles—the U.S. Department of Labor projects an average growth rate of 20 percent for all occupations. Technical and service occupations will grow the fastest during the 1990-2005 period:

**PROJECTED EMPLOYMENT CHANGES IN
BROAD OCCUPATIONAL GROUPS, 1990-2005**

Occupational group	Total increase/decrease in new jobs	Percentage change
All occupations	38,851,000	+20
Services	7,403,000	+29
Administrative support	6,413,000	+13
Operators	5,449,000	+4
Marketing and sales	5,379,000	+24
Precision production	4,764,000	+13
Professional specialty	4,281,000	+32
Managerial	3,085,000	+27
Technicians	1,200,000	+37
Agriculture-related	863,000	+5

More than one-half of all job growth in the 1990-2005 period will be contributed by 30 fast growing occupations:

**FASTEST GROWING OCCUPATIONS CONTRIBUTING
MORE THAN 50% TO JOB GROWTH, 1990-2005**

Occupation	New jobs created
Sales workers, retail	887,000
Registered nurses	767,000
Cashiers	685,000
General office clerks	670,000
Truck drivers, light and heavy	617,000
General managers and top executives	598,000
Janitors and cleaners	555,000
Nursing aides, orderlies, and attendants	552,000
Food counter, fountain, and related workers	550,000
Waiters and waitresses	449,000
Teachers, secondary school	437,000
Receptionists and information clerks	422,000

- Systems analysts and computer scientists   366,000
- Food preparation workers   365,000
- Childcare workers   353,000
- Gardeners and groundskeepers   348,000
- Accountants and auditors   340,000
- Teachers, elementary school   313,000
- Guards   298,000
- Teachers aids and educational assistants   278,000
- Licensed practical nurses   269,000
- Clerical supervisors and managers   263,000
- Home health aids   263,000
- Maintenance repairers, general utility   251,000
- Secretaries except legal and medical   248,000
- Cooks, short order and fast food   246,000
- Stock clerks, sales floor   209,000
- Lawyers   206,000

The patterns of growth and decline in industries and occupations during the 1990s generally follow the larger changes in the economy we discussed earlier. The U.S. Department of Labor studies have identified the fastest growing and declining occupations for the years 1990-2005. Occupations, for example, contributing the largest job growth in terms of the actual number of new jobs generated will be in service industries requiring a wide range of skills. Nearly half of the 30 fastest growing occupations will be in the health services alone, and most of the jobs will require advanced education and training:

30 FASTEST GROWING
OCCUPATIONS, 1990-2005

Occupation	Percent growth
- Home health aides	92
- Paralegals	85
- Systems analysts and computer scientists	79
- Personal and home care aides	77
- Physical therapists	76
- Medical assistants	74
- Operations research analysts	73
- Human services workers	71
- Radiological technologists and technicians	70
- Medical secretaries	68
- Physical and corrective therapy assistants and aides	64
- Psychologists	64
- Travel agents	62
- Correction officers	61
- Data processing equipment repairers	60

- Flight attendants   59
- Computer programmers   56
- Occupational therapists   55
- Surgical technologists   55
- Medical records technicians   54
- Management analysts   52
- Respiratory therapists   52
- Childcare workers   49
- Marketing, advertising, and public relations managers   47
- Legal secretaries   47
- Receptionists and information clerks   47
- Registered nurses   44
- Nursing aides, orderlies, and attendants   43
- Licensed practical nurses   42
- Cooks, restaurant   42

On the other hand, nearly half of the 30 fastest declining occupations will be in declining industries affected by technological change:

30 FASTEST DECLINING
OCCUPATIONS, 1990-2005

Occupation	Numerical decline
Farmers	224,000
Bookkeeping, accounting, and auditing clerks	133,000
Childcare workers, private household	124,000
Sewing machine operators, garment	116,000
Electrical and electronic assemblers	105,000
Typists and word processors	103,000
Cleaners and servants, private household	101,000
Farmer workers	92,000
Electrical and electronic equipment assembler	81,000
Textile draw-out and winding machine operators	61,000
Switchboard operators	57,000
Machine forming operators	43,000
Machine tool cutting operators	42,000
Telephone and cable TV line installers and repairers	40,000
Central office and PBX installers and repairers	34,000
Central office operators	31,000
Statistical clerks	31,000
Packaging and filling machine operators	27,000
Station installers and repairers, telephone	26,000
Bank tellers	25,000
Lathe turning machine tool setters	20,000
Grinders and polishers, hand	19,000
Electromechanical equipment assemblers	18,000
Grinding machine setters	18,000
Service station attendants	17,000

- Directory assistance operators   16,000
- Butchers and meatcutters   14,000
- Chemical equipment controllers   14,000
- Drilling and boring machine tool setters   13,000
- Meter readers, utilities   12,000

DETERMINE "THE BEST" JOBS FOR YOU

The fastest growing occupational fields are not necessarily the best ones to enter. For example, many of the fastest growing jobs—personal and home care aides, travel agents, childcare workers, flight attendants, nursing aids, cooks, receptionists, and information clerks—represent low paying jobs which provide little opportunity for improving earnings or advancing one's career.

The best job and career for you will depend on your particular work and lifestyle values. Money, for example, is only one of many determiners of whether or not a job and career is particularly desirable. A job may pay a great deal of money, but it also may be very stressful and insecure, or it is found in an undesirable location. "The best" job for you will be one you find very rewarding in terms of your own criteria and priorities.

Periodically some observers of the labor market attempt to identify what are the best, the worst, the hottest, the most lucrative, or the most promising jobs and careers of the decade. The latest and most objective attempt to assemble a list of "the best" jobs in America is presented in the 1992 edition of Les Krantz's *The Jobs Rated Almanac*. Similar in methodology to *The Places Rated Almanac* for identifying the best places to live in America, *The Jobs Rated Almanac* evaluates and ranks 250 jobs in terms of six primary "job quality" criteria: work environment, security, stress, income, outlook, and physical demands. According to his analysis, the 50 highest ranking jobs by accumulated score of these criteria are:

"THE BEST" JOBS IN AMERICA

Job title	Overall rank	Cumulative score
Software Engineer	1	56
Actuary	2	121
Computer Systems Analyst	3	124
Computer Programmer	4	228
Mathematician	5	235

- Accountant   6   277
- Meteorologist   7   297
- Biologist   8   299
- Motion Picture Editor   9   307
- Sociologist   10   308
- Pharmacist   11   312
- Hospital Administrator   12   313
- Paralegal Assistant   13   330
- Parole Officer   14   343
- Physiologist   15   351
- Judge (Federal)   16   353
- Medical Secretary   17   362
- Industrial Engineer   18   370
- Urban/Regional Planner   19   375
- Electrical Engineer   20   384
- Guidance/Employment Counselor   21   385
- Optometrist   22   389
- Historian   23   390
- Astrologer   23   390
- Aerospace Engineer   25   397
- Statistician   26   401
- Medical Records Technician   27   403
- Publication Editor   28   414
- Medical Technologist   29   420
- Civil Engineer   30   424
- Psychologist   31   425
- Bank Officer   32   427
- Computer Service Technician   33   428
- Podiatrist   34   430
- Mechanical Engineer   35   438
- Postal Inspector   36   444
- Medical Laboratory Technician   37   453
- Protestant Minister   38   455
- Nuclear Engineer   39   461
- Political Scientist   40   462
- Chiropractor   1   464
- Optician   42   468
- Audiologist   42   468
- Broadcast Technician   44   470
- Occupational Therapist   45   472
- Industrial Designer   46   483
- Agricultural Scientist   47   484
- Speech Pathologist   48   487
- Petroleum Engineer   49   488
- Attorney   50   490

For the relative rankings of the remaining 200 jobs as well as the ratings of each job on individual criterion, consult the latest edition of *The Jobs Rated Almanac*, which should be available in your local library or bookstore. It can also be ordered from Impact Publications by completing the order form at the end of this book.

These 50 "best" jobs evaluated according to six criteria differ from the 50 ranked according to income and outlook:

Rank	INCOME	OUTLOOK
1	Basketball Player (NBA)	Software Engineer
2	Baseball Player (Major league)	Computer Systems Analyst
3	Football Player (NFL)	Psychologist
4	Surgeon	Military (Commissioned Officer)
5	Physician (General Practice)	Computer Service Technician
6	Symphony Conductor	Highway Patrol Officer
7	Osteopath	Attorney
8	Psychiatrist	Surgeon
9	Attorney	Podiatrist
10	Stockbroker	Accountant
11	Airplane Pilot	Correction Officer
12	Optometrist	Physician (General Practice)
13	Race Car Driver (Indy Class)	Psychiatrist
14	Orthodontist	Chiropractor
15	Dentist	Hospital Administrator
16	Basketball Coach (NCAA)	Actuary
17	Baseball Umpire (Major League)	Judge (Federal)
18	Chiropractor	Optometrist
19	Podiatrist	Guidance/EmploymentCounselor
20	Electrical Engineer	Protestant Minister
21	Petroleum Engineer	Electrical Engineer
22	Newscaster	Respiratory Therapist
23	Meteorologist	Advertising Account Executive
24	Mechanical Engineer	Undertaker
25	Nuclear Engineer	Computer Programmer
26	Industrial Engineer	Symphony Conductor
27	Rabbi	Astronaut
28	Aerospace Engineer	Parole Officer
29	Geologist	Airline Pilot
30	Actuary	Sociologist
31	Civil Engineer	Military (Enlisted Person)
32	President (U.S.)	Motion Picture Editor
33	Motion Picture Editor	Occupational Therapist
34	Hotel Manager	Meteorologist
35	Astronaut	Medical Secretary
36	Judge (Federal)	Dentist
37	Software Engineer	Basketball Coach (NCAA)
38	Economist	Veterinarian
39	Computer Systems Analyst	Nurse (Registered)
40	Sociologist	Biologist

41	Chemist	College Professor
42	College Professor	Civil Engineer
43	Psychologist	Medical Technologist
44	Archeologist	Oceanographer
45	Anthropologist	Paralegal Assistant
46	Political Scientist	Osteopath
47	Fashion Model	Urban/Regional Planner
48	Historian	Personnel Recruiter
49	Zoologist	Geologist
50	Astronomer	Flight Attendant

100 "BEST" CAREERS FOR THE 21st CENTURY

Four other writers have attempted to identify the 100 or more best jobs and careers for the 1990s and into the 21st century. In *The 100 Best Jobs For the 1990s and Beyond*, for example, Carol Kleiman identifies—through a mixture of observations, interviews, and intuition—the following jobs as the "best" in 10 career areas:

BUSINESS AND FINANCIAL SERVICES

- Accountant/Auditor
- Bank Loan Officer
- Corporate Financial Analyst
- Court Reporter
- Economist
- Financial Planner
- Insurance Claim Examiner
- Investment Banker
- Lawyer
- Management Consultant
- Paralegal
- Real Estate Agent/Broker
- Real Estate Appraiser
- Underwriter

EDUCATION, GOVERNMENT, AND SOCIAL SERVICES

- Corrections Officer/Guard/Jailer
- Educational Administrator
- Firefighter
- Librarian
- Mathematician/Statistician
- Police Officer
- Psychologist/Counselor
- Social Worker
- Teacher/Professor

ENGINEERING AND COMPUTER TECHNOLOGY

- Computer Operator
- Computer Programmer
- Computer Service Technician
- Computer Systems Analyst
- Database Manager
- Drafter
- Engineer
- Information Systems Manager
- Manufacturing Specialist (CAD/CAM and CAI)
- Operations Systems Research Analyst
- Peripheral Electronic Data Processing Equipment Operator

HEALTH CARE PROFESSIONS

- Dental Hygienist
- Dentist
- Dietitian
- Health Services Administrator
- Home Health Aide
- Licensed Practical Nurse
- Medical Records Administrator
- Occupational Therapist
- Ophthalmic Laboratory Technician
- Optician
- Paramedic
- Pharmacist
- Physical Therapist
- Physician
- Physician Assistant
- Podiatrist
- Radiologic Technologist
- Registered Nurse
- Speech Pathologist/Audiologist
- Veterinarian

HOSPITALITY INDUSTRY

- Cook/Chef
- Flight Attendant
- Flight Engineer
- Hotel Manager/Assistant
- Pilot
- Restaurant/Food Service Manager
- Travel Agent

MANAGEMENT AND OFFICE PERSONNEL

- Clerical Supervisor/Office Manager
- Corporate Personnel Trainer

- Employment Interviewer
- Human Resources Manager/Executive
- Labor Relations Specialist
- Secretary/Office Administrator

MANUFACTURING, REPAIR, CONSTRUCTION, AGRICULTURE, AND TRANSPORTATION

- Aircraft Technician
- Appliance/Power Tool Repairer
- Architect
- Automotive Mechanic
- Carpenter
- Farm Manager
- Industrial Designer
- Landscape Architect
- Office/Business Machine Repairer
- Operations Manager/Manufacturing
- Radio/TV Service Technician
- Truck Driver

MEDIA AND THE ARTS

- Actor/Director/Producer
- Advertising and Marketing Account Supervisor
- Arts Administrator
- Commercial and Graphic Artists
- Editor/Writer
- Interior Designer
- Photographer/Camera Operator
- Public Relations Specialist
- Radio/TV News Reporter
- Reporter/Correspondent

SALES AND PERSONAL SERVICES

- Cosmetologist
- Insurance Salesperson
- Retail Salesperson
- Wholesale Sales Representative

SCIENCE

- Agricultural Scientist
- Biological Scientist
- Chemist
- Environmental Scientist
- Food Scientist
- Physicist/Astronomer

Shelly Field similarly identifies in *100 Best Careers For the Year 2000* the fastest growing career areas for the coming decade:

MEDICAL TECHNOLOGY AND HEALTH CARE CAREERS

- Alcohol and Drug Abuse Counselor
- Chiropractor
- Clinical Laboratory Technologist
- Dance Therapist
- Dental Assistant
- Dental Hygienist
- Dentist
- Dietitian
- Dispensing Optician
- EEG Technologist/Technician
- EKG Technician
- Emergency Medical Technician
- Health Services Administrator
- Home Health Aide
- Licensed Practical Nurse (L.P.N.)
- Medical Records Technician
- Music Therapist
- Nurse's Aide
- Pharmacist
- Physical Therapist
- Physical Therapy Assistant
- Physician
- Physician Assistant
- Podiatrist
- Radiologic Technologist
- Registered Nurse (R.N.)
- Veterinarian
- Veterinary Technician

GERIATRICS CAREERS

- Geriatric Assessment Coordinator
- Geriatric Care Manager
- Geriatric Social Worker
- Nursing Home Activities Director
- Recreational Therapist
- Retirement Planner

COMPUTER CAREERS

- CAD Specialist
- Computer Operator
- Computer Programmer
- Computer Salesperson
- Computer Service Technician

- Computer Trainer
- Systems Analyst
- Technical Documentation Specialist
- Word Processor Operator

CONSERVATION AND ENVIRONMENTAL CAREERS

- County Extension Agriculture Agent
- Environmental Engineer
- Environmental Technician (water and wastewater)
- Hazardous Waste Management Technician

ADVERTISING, COMMUNICATIONS, AND PUBLIC RELATIONS CAREERS

- Advertising Art Director
- Copywriter
- Editor
- Graphic Artist
- Marketing Manager
- Public Relations Counselor
- Radio/Television Advertising Salesperson
- Reporter (print)

SALES AND SERVICE CAREERS

- Accountant
- Actuary
- Child-Care Worker
- Correction Officer
- Craftperson
- Hairstylist
- Insurance Sales Agent
- Law Enforcement Officer
- Lawyer
- Manufacturer's Representative
- Paralegal
- Personal Shopper
- Real Estate Agent
- Salesperson
- Secretary

HOSPITALITY AND TRAVEL

- Flight Attendant
- Hotel/Motel Manager
- Pilot
- Restaurant Manager
- Travel Agent

SCIENCE AND ENGINEERING CAREERS

- Biochemist
- Civil Engineer
- Mechanical Engineer
- Meteorologist

FITNESS AND NUTRITION CAREERS

- Aerobics Exercise Instructor
- Personal Trainer
- Sports and Fitness Nutritionist

EDUCATION CAREERS

- School Counselor
- Teacher

HOME-BASED BUSINESS CAREERS

- Adult Day Care Service
- Bed and Breakfast Inn Owner
- Bookkeeping and Accounting Service
- Catering Service
- Child-Care Service
- Cleaning Service
- Desktop Publishing Business
- Event Planning Service
- Gift Basket Service
- Home Instruction Service
- Image Consulting Service
- Information Broker Service
- Pet Setting Service
- Publicity Consulting Service
- Word Processing Service

Michael Harkavy in *101 Careers: A Guide to the Fastest-Growing Opportunities* identifies the top jobs for the 1990s according to nine major career categories:

ACCOUNTING, BANKING, FINANCE, INSURANCE, AND MANAGEMENT

- Accountants and auditors
- Actuaries
- Budget analysts
- Financial planners and managers
- Insurance agents and brokers
- Investment bankers
- Loan officers

- Management consultants
- Securities analysts
- Securities sales representatives (stockbrokers)

SALES AND MARKETING

- Advertising Managers and account executives
- Media planners
- Public relations specialists
- Purchasing agents and mangers
- Real estate agents and brokers
- Sales and marketing executives
- Wholesale and retail buyers

APPLIED SCIENCE: ARCHITECTURE, ENGINEERING AND COMPUTER SCIENCE

- Aerospace engineers
- Architects
- Chemical engineers
- Chief information officers
- Civil engineers
- Computer programmers
- Computer security specialists
- Computer systems analysts
- Electrical and electronics engineers
- Industrial engineers
- Mechanical engineers
- Metallurgical, ceramic, and materials engineers
- Nuclear engineers
- Surveyors

NATURAL SCIENCE AND MATHEMATICS

- Astronomers
- Biological scientists
- Chemists
- Geoscientists
- Mathematicians
- Meteorologists
- Physicists
- Science technicians

SOCIAL SCIENCES, THE LAW, AND LAW ENFORCEMENT

- Alcohol and drug counselors
- Attorneys
- Corporate trainers
- Economists
- Paralegals, or legal assistants
- Police, detectives, and special agents

- Psychologists
- Social workers
- Urban and regional planners

HEALTH CARE

- Chiropractors
- Clinical laboratory technologists and technicians
- Dental hygienists
- Dentists
- Dietitians and nutritionists
- Dispensing opticians
- EEG technologists and technicians
- EKG technicians
- Emergency medical technicians
- Exercise physiologists
- Health services administrators
- Industrial hygienists
- Licensed practical nurses
- Medical record technicians
- Nuclear medicine technologists
- Occupational therapists
- Optometrists
- Pharmacists
- Pharmacy technicians
- Physical therapists
- Physician assistants
- Physicians
- Podiatrists
- Radiologic technologists
- Registered nurses
- Respiratory therapists
- Speech-language pathologists and audiologists
- Veterinarians

EDUCATION AND LIBRARY SCIENCE

- Adult and vocational education teachers
- Archivists and curators
- College and university faculty
- Educational administrators
- Elementary school teachers
- Guidance counselors
- Librarians
- Preschool and childcare workers
- Secondary school teachers

ARTS, ENTERTAINMENT, AND MEDIA

- Actors, directors, and producers
- Broadcast technicians

- Dancers and choreographers
- Editors—books and magazines
- Graphic artists
- Musicians
- Photographers
- Radio and TV announcers and broadcasters
- Reporters and correspondents
- Translators and interpreters

AIR TRANSPORTATION

- Aircraft mechanics
- Aircraft pilots
- Air traffic controllers
- Flight attendants
- Travel agents

Finally, Nicholas Basta in *Top Professions* identifies what he believes are the 100 most popular, dynamic, and profitable careers for the 1990s:

FINANCE, INSURANCE, AND BANKING

- Bank officer
- Financial analyst
- Financial information researcher
- Financial planner/tax adviser
- Insurance agent
- Investment banker
- Risk manager
- Stockbroker
- Underwriter and actuary

BUSINESS, PUBLIC ADMINISTRATION, AND CONSULTING

- Accountant
- Association executive
- Business consultant
- Cost estimator
- Human resources manager
- Import/export trade manager
- Operations/systems researcher
- Public administrator
- Purchasing agent
- Telecommunications specialist

LAWYERS, LAW ENFORCEMENT, AND SECURITY

- Corporate lawyer
- Detective, private, or government

- Lawyer
- Paralegal/law office manager
- Police officer
- Security specialist

MARKETING AND SALES

- Consumer product manager
- Franchise manager
- Industrial product manager
- Market researcher
- Marketing manager
- Retail buyer

THE HARD SCIENCES

- Agricultural and food scientist
- Biologist
- Chemist
- Mathematician/statistician
- Physicist
- Veterinarian

TRAVEL AND TRANSPORTATION

- Airline pilot
- Conference/meeting planner
- Corporate shipping manager
- Travel agent

REAL ESTATE MANAGEMENT

- Architect
- Building manager
- Developer
- Real estate broker
- Urban planner

EARTH SCIENCE AND FARMING

- Environmental technologist
- Farm manager
- Geoscientist
- Landscape architect

THE SOCIAL SCIENCES AND SERVICES

- Economist
- Job counselor/recruiter
- Psychologist
- Recreational worker and therapist

- Social worker

ENGINEERING AND TECHNOLOGY

- Aerospace engineer
- Chemical engineer
- Civil engineer
- Electrical/electronics engineer
- Energy engineer
- Engineering/industrial technologist
- Industrial/manufacturing engineer
- Laboratory specialist
- Mechanical engineer
- Metallurgical and materials engineer

COMPUTERS AND DATA PROCESSING

- Computer engineer
- Computer programmer
- Library scientist/information broker
- Management information systems (MIS) specialist
- Systems analyst
- Technical services specialist

MEDICAL PROFESSIONS

- Dentist
- Hospital administrator
- Industrial hygienist
- Medical doctor
- Optometrist
- Pharmacist
- Registered dietitian/nutritionist
- Registered nurse
- Therapist

TEACHING

- College administrator
- College professor
- Corporate training specialist
- Elementary and secondary school teacher

ADVERTISING AND PUBLIC RELATIONS

- Advertising account executive
- Copywriter
- Media planner
- Public relations specialist

ARTS AND MEDIA

- Commercial artist
- Designer
- Journalist
- Media producer
- Musician
- Photographer/cinematographer
- Radio/TV announcer

LEISURE, EATING, AND SPORTS

- Hotel administrator
- Restaurant chef
- Restaurant manager
- Sports/recreation manager

These predictions should be examined with some degree of caution since many of the predictions are likely to be inaccurate.

SIMILARITIES AND DIFFERENCES

What is common and different about these predictions and projections? First, most are based upon data and analyses provided by the U.S. Department of Labor. Accordingly, they reflect the economic assumptions of the U.S. Department of Labor's planning model—steady-state economic growth. They do not, nor are they able to, incorporate what has become a pattern for most predictions during the past two decades—uncertainty attendant with recessionary cycles and unique events. As such, they should be examined with some degree of caution since many of the predictions are likely to be inaccurate due to the uncertain nature of future economic developments and the continuing restructuring of the economy.

Second, most writers identify a similar set of jobs and careers for the coming decade, no doubt based upon the U.S. Department of

Labor's labor market data and economic projections. Indeed, nearly 80 percent of the so-called "best" jobs for the 1990s are repeated on others' lists of the "best" jobs. This remarkable degree of consensus and redundancy argues for serious examination of these similar lists.

Third, most differences lie in categorizing the major career areas —seven versus nine or ten different areas—which identify the "best" jobs. In the end, the career categories are very similar, as are the jobs identified.

Finally, several questionable jobs and careers appear on some of these lists. They question the credibility of the writers' research. Indeed, it is difficult to believe that jobs such as a home health aide, word processor operator, and personal shopper are good jobs since they are either low paying jobs that lead to little or no career advancement or declining occupations. Jobs such as the President of the U.S., NBA basketball player, and an NCAA basketball coach are so limited in number as to be useless information for most individuals who have little or no chance of ever attaining such positions.

LOOK FOR EXCITING NEW
OCCUPATIONS IN THE 21st CENTURY

In the early 1980s the auto and related industries—steel, rubber, glass, aluminum, railroads and auto dealers—accounted for one-fifth of all employment in the United States. Today that percentage continues to decline as service occupations further dominate America's occupational structure.

New occupations for the 1990s and beyond will center around information, energy, high-tech, health care, and financial industries. They promise to create a new occupational structure and vocabulary relating to computers, robotics, biotechnology, lasers, and fiber optics. And as these fields begin to apply new technologies to developing new innovations, they in turn will generate other new occupations in the 21st century. While most new occupations are not major growth fields, because they do not initially generate a large number of new jobs, they will present individuals with fascinating new opportunities to become leaders in pioneering new fields and industries.

Futurists identify several emerging occupations for the coming decades. Most tend to brainstorm lists of occupational titles they feel will emerge in the next decade based on present trends. Others identify additional occupations which may be created from new, unforeseen technological breakthroughs. Feingold and Miller (*Emerging Careers*), for example, see 30 new careers emerging:

EMERGING CAREERS FOR
THE 21st CENTURY

- artificial intelligence technician
- aquaculturist
- automotive fuel cell battery technician
- benefits analyst
- bionic electron technician
- computational linguist
- computer microprocessor
- cryonics technician
- dialysis technologist
- electronic mail technician
- fiber optic technician
- fusion engineer
- hazardous waste technician
- horticulture therapy
- image consultant
- information broker
- information center manager
- job developer
- leisure consultant
- materials utilization specialist
- medical diagnostic imaging technician
- myotherapist
- relocation counselor
- retirement counselor
- robot technician
- shyness consultant
- software club director
- space mechanic
- underwater archaeologist
- water quality specialist

Most futurists agree that such new occupations will have two dominant characteristics during the 1990s and into the 21st century:

- **They will generate a small number of new jobs** in comparison to the overall growth of jobs in hundreds of more traditional service fields, such as sales workers, office clerks, truck drivers, and janitors.

- **They require a high level of education and skills** for entry into the fields as well as continuing training and retraining as each field transforms itself into additional growth fields.

If you plan to pursue any of these occupations, expect to first acquire highly specialized skills which may require years of higher education and training.

CONSIDER THE IMPLICATIONS
OF FUTURE TRENDS FOR YOU

Most growth industries and occupations require skills training and experience. Moving into one of these fields will require knowledge of job qualifications, the nature of the work, and sources of employment. Fortunately, the U.S. Department of Labor publishes several useful sources of information available in most libraries to help you. These include the *Dictionary of Occupational Titles*, which identifies over 13,000 job titles. The *Occupational Outlook Handbook* provides an overview of current labor market conditions and projections as well as discusses nearly 250 occupations that account for 107 million jobs, or 87 percent of the nation's total jobs, according to several useful informational categories: nature of work; working conditions; employment; training, other qualifications, and achievement; job outlook; earnings; related occupations; and sources of additional information. Anyone seeking to enter the job market or change careers should initially consult these publications for information on trends and occupations.

However, remember that labor market statistics reflect trends for industries and occupations **as a whole**. They reveal little about the shift in employment emphasis **within the industry**, and nothing about the outlook of particular jobs for you, **the individual**. For example, employment in agriculture is expected to decline by 14 percent between 1985 and 2000, but the decline consists of an important shift in employment emphasis within the industry: there will be 500,000 fewer self-employed workers but 150,000 more wage and salary earners in the service end of agriculture. The employment statistics also assume a steady-state of economic growth with consumers having more and more disposable income to stimulate a wide variety of service and trade industries.

Therefore, be careful in how you interpret and use this information in making your own job and career decisions. If, for example, you want to become a college teacher, and the data indeed tells you there will be a 10 percent decline in this occupation during the next 10 years, this does not mean you could not find employment, as well as advance, in this field. It merely means that, on the whole, competition may be keen for these jobs, and that future advancement and mobility in this occupation may not be very good—on the whole. At the same time, there may be numerous job opportunities available in a declining occupational field as many individuals abandon the field for more attractive occupations. In fact, you may do much better in this declining occupation than in a growing field depending on your interests, motivations, abilities, job search savvy, and level of competition. And if the 1990s become a decade of boom and bust cycles, expect most of these U.S. Department of Labor statistics and projections to be invalid for the economic realities of this decade.

As we emphasized earlier, use this industrial and occupational data to expand your awareness of various job and career options. By no means should you make critical education, training, and occupational choices based upon this information alone.

THE BEST JOBS FOR YOU

We've included this information on the best jobs for 1990s and into the 21st century so you can broaden your job vocabulary as well as survey different jobs that might be relevant to your own interests and skills. Knowing how economic and job trends can change dramatically, we do not recommend making definitive career choices based only on this type of predictive information. Therefore, you must be cautious in how you interpret and use this information.

What is certain is that many of the so-called "best" jobs for the future will require major investments of education and training. These jobs require skilled individuals who are willing to acquire education and training necessary for taking advantage of new opportunities that arise in the future.

As we will see in subsequent chapters, the best jobs for you are ones that best "fit" your interests, skills, and abilities. If you wish to survey several of the jobs outlined in this chapter, we recommend surveying the bibliography in Chapter Fifteen and the career resource section at the end of this book. Numerous resources are available to provide in-depth information on the nature of work, working conditions, job outlook, education and training requirements, and salaries relevant to hundreds of different occupations and jobs. For a quick overview of these jobs, we recommend examining our other book, *The Best Jobs For the 1990s and Into the 21st Century,* as well as the latest edition of the U.S. Department of Labor's *Occupational Outlook Handbook.* These books will provide you with a great deal of information on alternative jobs and careers and hopefully generate numerous ideas relevant to your career future.

Chapter Three

TEST YOUR CAREERING COMPETENCIES

Doing first things first requires some basic self-knowledge about your capabilities to conduct an effective job search. Do you, for example, know what your major strengths are and how to communicate them to potential employers? Do you know which jobs are ideally suited for your particular skills and motivations? Can you develop a one to two-page resume that clearly communicates your qualifications to employers? How well can you plan and implement a job search that will lead to several interviews and a job offer that is right for you? We need to first address these questions prior to examining your interests, values, abilities, skills, motivations, and goals.

CAREERING COMPETENCIES

Knowing **where** the jobs are is important to your job search. But knowing **how to find a job** is even more important. Before you acquire names, addresses, and phone numbers of potential employers, you should possess the necessary job search knowledge and skills for gathering and using job information effectively.

Answers to many of your job related questions are found by

examining your present level of job search knowledge and skills. Successful job seekers, for example, use a great deal of information as well as specific skills and strategies for getting the jobs they want.

Let's begin by testing for the level of job search information, skills, and strategies you currently possess as well as those you need to develop and improve. You can easily identify your level of job search competence by completing the following exercise:

YOUR CAREERING COMPETENCIES

INSTRUCTIONS: Respond to each statement by circling which number at the right best represents your situation.

SCALE: 1 = strongly agree
          2 = agree
          3 = maybe, not certain
          4 = disagree
          5 = strongly disagree

1. I know what motivates me to excel at work. 1 2 3 4 5

2. I can identify my strongest abilities and skills. 1 2 3 4 5

3. I have seven major achievements that clarify a pattern of interests and abilities that are relevant to my job and career. 1 2 3 4 5

4. I know what I both like and dislike in work. 1 2 3 4 5

5. I know what I want to do during the next 10 years. 1 2 3 4 5

6. I have a well defined career objective that focuses my job search on particular organizations and employers. 1 2 3 4 5

7. I know what skills I can offer employers in different occupations. 1 2 3 4 5

8. I know what skills employers most seek in candidates. 1 2 3 4 5

9. I can clearly explain to employers what I do well and enjoy doing. 1 2 3 4 5

10. I can specify why an employer should hire me. 1 2 3 4 5

11. I can gain support of family and friends for
    making a job or career change.   1 2 3 4 5

12. I can find 10 to 20 hours a week to conduct
    a part-time job search.   1 2 3 4 5

13. I have the financial ability to sustain a three-
    month job search.   1 2 3 4 5

14. I can conduct library and interview research
    on different occupations, employers,
    organizations, and communities.   1 2 3 4 5

15. I can write different types of effective resumes,
    job search letters, and thank you notes.   1 2 3 4 5

16. I can produce and distribute resumes and
    letters to the right people.   1 2 3 4 5

17. I can list my major accomplishments
    in action terms.   1 2 3 4 5

18. I can identify and target employees I want to
    interview.   1 2 3 4 5

19. I can develop a job referral network.   1 2 3 4 5

20. I can persuade others to join in forming a
    job search support group.   1 2 3 4 5

21. I can prospect for job leads.   1 2 3 4 5

22. I can use the telephone to develop prospects
    and get referrals and interviews.   1 2 3 4 5

23. I can plan and implement an effective
    direct-mail job search campaign.   1 2 3 4 5

24. I can generate one job interview for every
    10 job search contacts I make.   1 2 3 4 5

25. I can follow-up on job interviews.   1 2 3 4 5

26. I can negotiate a salary 10-20% above
    what an employer initially offers.   1 2 3 4 5

27. I can persuade an employer to renegotiate
    my salary after six months on the job.   1 2 3 4 5

28. I can create a position for myself in
    an organization.   1 2 3 4 5

29. I have a positive and optimistic view
    of my career future in the decade ahead.   1 2 3 4 5

30. I know which jobs offer the best
    opportunities in the decade ahead.   1 2 3 4 5

TOTALS _____

GRAND TOTAL _____

ADDING IT UP

You can calculate your overall careering competencies by adding the numbers you circled for a composite scale. If your grand total is more than 85 points, you need to work on developing your careering skills. How you scored each item will indicate to what degree you need to work on improving specific job search skills. If your score is under 50 points, you are well on your way toward job search success. In either case, this book should help you better focus your job search as well as identify job search skills you need to acquire or strengthen.

Chapter Four

EMPOWERMENT THROUGH THE JOB FINDING PROCESS

How do you go about finding the best job for you? Join us as we outline an approach that works well for thousands of successful job seekers each year. The approach is based upon the notion of **empowerment**—you have within you the power to achieve your career goals. But you must do first things first before initiating the most important steps in your job search.

EMPOWERMENT COMES BY WAY OF A PROCESS

Finding your best job requires that you (1) know who you are, (2) where you want to go, and (3) how to get there. This involves an important process of moving from an initial stage of self-awareness to several other action stages involving specific job search activities that eventually result in employment.

If you have a clear understanding of each element and relationship within this process, you should be in a better position to know who you are and where you want to go. By relating each element to the other, the process becomes a crucial blueprint revealing how to get where you want to go.

FINDING JOBS

If you are looking for your first job, reentering the job market after a lengthy absence, or planning a job or career change, you will join millions of individuals who engage in the same careering activities each year. Indeed, more than 20 million people find themselves unemployed each year. Millions of others try to increase their satisfaction within the workplace as well as advance their careers by looking for alternative jobs and careers. If you are like most workers, you will make more than 10 job changes and between 3 and 5 career changes during your lifetime.

But how do you make such changes? Do you look for jobs in a well thought-out and planned manner or do new jobs come to you by accident? Most people make job or career transitions by accident. They do little other than take advantage of opportunities that may arise unexpectedly.

While chance and luck do play important roles in finding employment, we recommend that you **plan** for future job and career changes so that you will experience even greater degrees of chance and luck!

A career is a series of related jobs which have common skill, interest, and motivational bases.

Finding a job or changing a career in a systematic and well-planned manner is hard yet rewarding work. The task should first be based on a clear understanding of the key ingredients that define jobs and careers. Starting with this understanding, you should next convert key concepts into action steps for implementing your job search.

A career is a series of related jobs which have common skill, interest, and motivational bases. You may change jobs several times without changing careers. But once you change skills, interests, and motivations, you change careers.

It's not easy to find a job given the present structure of the job market. Although it projects an outward appearance of coherence, the job market is relatively disorganized. If you seek comprehensive, accurate, and timely job information, the job market will frustrate you with its poor communication. While you will find many employment services ready to assist you, such services tend to be fragmented and their performance is often disappointing; some are simply fraudulent, preying on highly motivated yet naive job seekers. Many career counselors espouse job search methods that are controversial; many are ineffective.

No system is organized to give people jobs. At best **you will encounter a highly decentralized and fragmented job finding system** consisting of job listings in newspapers, trade journals, employment offices, or computerized job data banks—all designed to link potential candidates with available job openings. Many people will try to sell you job information as well as questionable job search services, including testing and assessment exercises that you can easily do on your own with the help of this book! While efforts are underway to create a nationwide computerized job bank which would list available job vacancies on a daily basis, don't expect such data to become available soon nor to be very useful. Many of the listed jobs may be nonexistent, at a low skill and salary level, or represent only a few employers.

In the end, most systems organized to help you find a job do not provide you with the information you need in order to land the job that is most related to your skills and interests.

THE CAREER
DEVELOPMENT PROCESS

Finding a job is both an art and a science; it encompasses a variety of basic facts, principles, and skills which can be learned but which also must be adapted to individual situations. Thus, **learning how to find a job** can be as important to career success as **knowing how to perform a job**. Indeed, job finding skills are often more important to career success than job performance or work-content skills.

Our understanding of how to find jobs and change careers is illustrated on pages 53 and 54. As outlined on page 53, you should involve yourself in a four-step career development process as you prepare to move from one job to another.

THE CAREER DEVELOPMENT PROCESS

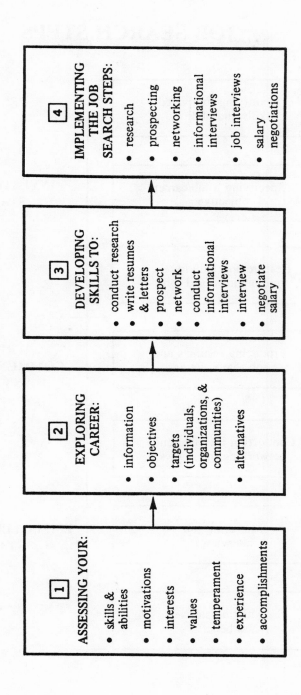

1 ASSESSING YOUR:

- skills & abilities
- motivations
- interests
- values
- temperament
- experience
- accomplishments

2 EXPLORING CAREER:

- information
- objectives
- targets (individuals, organizations, & communities)
- alternatives

3 DEVELOPING SKILLS TO:

- conduct research
- write resumes & letters
- prospect
- network
- conduct informational interviews
- interview
- negotiate salary

4 IMPLEMENTING THE JOB SEARCH STEPS:

- research
- prospecting
- networking
- informational interviews
- job interviews
- salary negotiations

JOB SEARCH STEPS

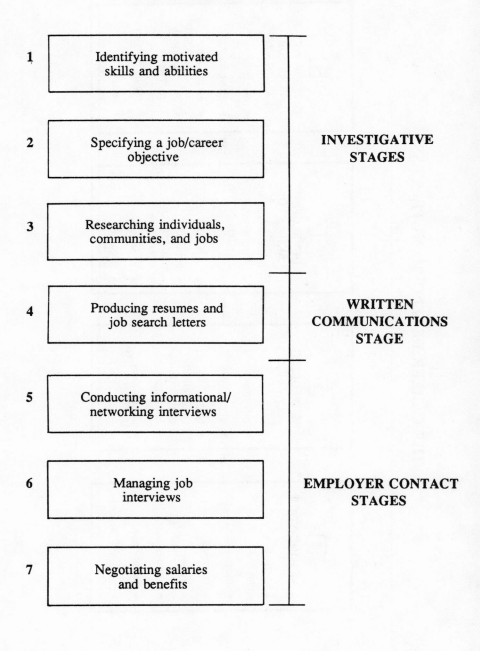

1. Identifying motivated skills and abilities

2. Specifying a job/career objective

3. Researching individuals, communities, and jobs

INVESTIGATIVE STAGES

4. Producing resumes and job search letters

WRITTEN COMMUNICATIONS STAGE

5. Conducting informational/networking interviews

6. Managing job interviews

7. Negotiating salaries and benefits

EMPLOYER CONTACT STAGES

FOUR STEP CAREER
DEVELOPMENT PROCESS

1. Conduct a self-assessment:

This first step involves assessing your skills, abilities, motivations, interests, values, temperaments, experience, and accomplishments—the major concern of this book. Your basic strategy is to develop a firm foundation of information on **yourself** before proceeding to other stages in the career development process. This self-assessment develops the necessary self-awareness upon which you can effectively communicate your qualifications to employers as well as focus and build your career.

2. Gather career and job information:

Closely related to the first step, this second step is an exploratory, research phase of your career development. Here you need to formulate goals, gather information about alternative jobs and careers through reading and talking to informed people, and then narrow your alternatives to specific job targets.

3. Develop job search skills:

The third step focuses your career around specific job search skills for landing the job you want. As further outlined on page 54, these job search skills are closely related to one another as a series of **job search steps**. They involve conducting research, writing resumes and letters, prospecting and networking, conducting informational interviews, interviewing for a job, and negotiating salary and terms of employment. Each of these job search skills involves well-defined strategies and tactics you must learn in order to be effective in the job market.

4. Implement each job search step:

The final career development step emphasizes the importance of transforming understanding into **action**. You do
this by implementing each job search step which already
incorporates the knowledge, skills, and abilities you acquired in Steps 1, 2, and 3.

ORGANIZE AND SEQUENCE YOUR JOB SEARCH

The figure on page 54 further expands our career development
process by examining the key elements in a successful job search. It
consists of a seven-step process which relates your past, present, and
future. The first two steps are outlined in this book. The remaining
steps are examined in several of our other books that deal with resumes, letters, networking, interviews, and salary negotiations (see
Chapter Fifteen).

Based on this concept, **your past** is well integrated into the
process of finding a job or changing your career. Therefore, you
should feel comfortable conducting your job search: it represents the
best of what you are in terms of your past and present accomplishments as these relate to your present and future goals. If you base
your job search on this process concept, you will communicate your
best self to employers as well as focus on **your strengths** both during
the job search and on the job.

Since the individual job search steps are interrelated, they should
be followed in sequence. If you fail to properly complete the initial
self-assessment steps, your job search may become haphazard,
aimless, and costly. For example, you should never write a resume
(Step 3) before first conducting an assessment of your skills (Step 1)
and identifying your objective (Step 2). Relating Step 1 to Step 2 is
especially critical to the successful implementation of all other job
search steps. You **must** complete Steps 1 and 2 **before** continuing on
to the other steps. Steps 3 to 6 may be conducted simultaneously
because they complement and reinforce one another.

Try to sequence your job search as close to these steps as possible.
The true value of this sequencing will become very apparent as you
implement your plan.

The processes and steps identified on pages 53 and 54 represent the careering and re-careering processes we and others have used successfully with thousands of clients during the past 30 years. They are equally applicable to the job market of the 1990s as long as you recognize the importance of acquiring work-content skills along with job search skills. You must do much more than just know how to find a job. In the job markets of today and tomorrow, you need to constantly review your work-content skills to make sure they are appropriate for the changing job market. Once you have acquired the necessary skills through training and retraining, you will be ready to target your skills on particular jobs and careers that you do well and enjoy doing. You will be able to avoid the trap of trying to fit into jobs that are not conducive to your particular mix of interests, abilities, skills, and motivations.

Chapter Five

SEEK PROFESSIONAL ASSISTANCE WHEN NECESSARY

Some people successfully conduct a job search based on the advice of books such as this. However, many others also need the assistance of various professional groups that offer specific career planning and job search services. These groups offer everything from testing and assessment services to making contacts with potential employers, including job vacancy information and temporary employment services. Some do one-on-one career counseling while others sponsor one to three-day workshops or six to twelve-week courses on the various steps in the career planning process.

You should know something about these services before you invest your time and money beyond this and other career planning and job search books.

OPTIONS

You have two options in organizing your job search. First, you can follow the principles and advice outlined in this and many other self-directed books. Just read the chapters and then put them into practice by following the step-by-step instructions. Second, you may wish to seek professional help to either supplement or replace this book. Indeed, many people will read parts of this book—perhaps all of it—and do nothing. Unwilling to take initiative, lacking sufficient time or motivation, or failing to follow-through, many people will eventually seek professional help to organize and implement their job search. They will pay good money to get someone else to tell them to follow the advice found in this book. Some people need this type of expensive motivation.

At the same time, we recognize the value of professional assistance. Especially with the critical assessment and objective setting steps (Chapters Seven through Eleven), some individuals may need more assistance than our advice and exercises provide. You may, for example, want to take a battery of tests to better understand your interests and values in relation to the workplace. And still others, due to a combination of job loss, failed relationships, or depression, may need therapy best provided by a trained psychologist or psychiatrist rather than career testing and information services provided by career counselors. If any of these situations pertain to you, by all means seek professional help.

POTENTIAL PITFALLS

You also should beware of pitfalls in seeking professional advice. While many services are excellent, other services are useless and fraudulent. Remember, career planning and job assistance are big businesses involving millions of dollars each year. Many people enter these businesses without expertise. Professional certification in these areas is extremely weak to non-existent in some states. Indeed, many so-called "professionals" get into the business because they are unemployed. In other words, they major in their own problem! Others are frauds and hucksters who prey on vulnerable and naive people who feel they need a "specialist" or "expert" to get them a job. They will take your money in exchange for broken promises. You will find several services promising to assist you in finding all types of jobs. You should know something about these professional services before you venture beyond this book.

If you are interested in exploring the services of job specialists, begin by looking in the Yellow Pages of your telephone directory under these headings: Management Consultants, Employment, Resumes, Career Planning, and Social Services. Several career planning and employment services are available, ranging from highly generalized to very specific services. Most services claim they can help you. If you read this book, you will be in a better position to seek out specific services as well as ask the right questions for screening the services. You may even discover you know more about finding a job than many of the so-called professionals!

> ## *While many services are excellent, other services are useless and fraudulent.*

ALTERNATIVE SERVICES

At least 10 different career planning and employment services are available to assist you with your job search. Each has certain advantages and disadvantages. Approach them with caution. Never sign a contract before you read the fine print, get a second opinion, and talk to former clients about the **results** they achieved through the service. With these words of caution in mind, let's take a look at the variety of services available.

1. Public employment services:

Public employment services usually consist of a state agency which provides employment assistance as well as dispenses unemployment compensation benefits. Employment assistance largely consists of job listings and counseling services. However, counseling services often screen individuals for employers who list with the public employment agency. If you are looking for entry-level jobs in the $10,000 to $18,000 range, contact this service. Most employers do not list with this service, especially for positions paying more than $20,000 a year. If you walk through one of these offices, you will find that most people are unemployed. Some experts believe these offices should be closed because they exacerbate unemployment;

they take people away from the more productive channels for employment—personal contacts—and put them in a line where they waste time and meet few helpful and positive people. Nonetheless many of these offices do offer useful employment services, including self-assessment and job search workshops as well as job banks that match skills and experience with available job vacancies. Go see for yourself if your state employment office offers useful services for you.

2. Private employment agencies:

Private employment agencies work for money, either from applicants or employers. Approximately 8,000 such agencies operate nationwide. Many are highly specialized in technical, scientific, and financial fields. The majority of these firms serve the interests of employers since employers—not applicants—represent repeat business. While employers normally pay the placement fee, many agencies charge applicants 10 to 15 percent of their first year salary. These firms have one major advantage: job leads which you may have difficulty uncovering elsewhere. Especially for highly specialized fields, a good firm can be extremely helpful. The major disadvantages are that they can be costly and the quality of the firms varies. Be careful in how you deal with them. Make sure you understand the fee structure and what they will do for you before you sign anything.

3. College/university placement offices:

College and university placement offices provide in-house career planning services for graduating students. While some give assistance to alumni, don't expect too much help if you have already graduated. Many of these offices are understaffed or provide only rudimentary services, such as maintaining a career planning library, coordinating on-campus interviews for graduating seniors, and conducting workshops on how to write resumes and interview. Others provide a full range of well supported services including testing and one-on-one counseling. Indeed, many community colleges offer such services to members of the community on a walk-in basis. You can use their libraries and computerized career assessment programs, take personality and interest inventories, or attend special workshops or full-semester career planning courses which will take you through each step of the career planning and job search processes. You are well advised to enroll in such a course since it is likely to provide just enough structure and content to assess your motivated abilities and skills and to assist you in implementing a successful job search plan. Check with your local campus to see what services you might use.

4. Private career and job search firms:

Private career and job search firms help individuals acquire job search skills. They do not find you a job. In other words, they teach you much—maybe more but possibly less—of what is outlined in this book. Expect to pay anywhere from $1,500 to $10,000 for this service. If you need a structured environment for conducting your job search, contract with one of these firms. One of the most popular firms is Haldane Associates. Many of their pioneering career planning and job search methods are incorporated in this book. You will find branches of this nationwide firm in many major cities.

5. Executive search firms and headhunters:

Executive search firms work for employers in finding employees to fill critical positions in the $40,000 plus salary range. They also are called "headhunters," "management consultants," and "executive recruiters." These firms play an important role in linking high level technical and managerial talent to organizations. Don't expect to contract for these services. Executive recruiters work for employers—not applicants. If a friend or relative is in this business or you have relevant skills of interest to these firms, let them know you are available—and ask for their advice. On the other hand, you may want to contact firms that specialize in recruiting individuals with your skill specialty. Several books identify how you can best approach "headhunters" on your own: *How to Select and Use an Executive Search Firm* (A. R. Taylor); *How to Answer a Headhunter's Call* (Robert H. Perry); *The Headhunter Strategy* (Kenneth J. Cole); *The Directory of Executive Recruiters* (Kennedy Publications); and *How to Get a Headhunter to Call* (Howard S. Freedman).

6. Marketing services:

Marketing services represent an interesting combination of job search and executive search activities. They can cost $2,500 or more, and they work with individuals anticipating a starting salary of at least $40,000 but preferably over $60,000. These firms try to minimize the time and risk of applying for jobs. A typical operation begins with a client paying a $150 fee for developing psychological, skills, and interests profiles. Next, a marketing plan is outlined and a contract signed for specific services. Using word processing equipment, the firm normally develops a slick "professional" resume and mails it along with a cover letter, to hundreds—maybe thousands—of firms. Clients are then briefed and sent to interview with interested employers. While you can save money and achieve the same results on your own, these firms do have one major advantage. They save you **time** by doing most of the work for you. Again, approach these services with caution and with the knowledge that you can probably do just as well—if not better—on your own by following the step-by-step advice of this and other jobs search books.

7. Women's Centers and special career services:

Women's Centers and special career services have been established to respond to the employment needs of special groups. Women's Centers are particularly active in sponsoring career planning workshops and job information networks. These centers tend to be geared toward elementary job search activities, because their clientele largely consists of housewives who are entering or re-entering the workforce with little knowledge of the job market. Special career services arise at times for different categories of employees. For example, many unemployed aerospace engineers, teachers, veterans, air traffic controllers, and government employees have formed special groups for developing job search skills and sharing job leads.

8. Testing and assessment centers:

Testing and assessment centers provide assistance for identifying vocational skills, interests, and objectives. Usually staffed by trained professionals, these centers administer several types of tests and charge from $300 to $800 per person. You may wish to use some of these services if you feel our activities in Chapters Six through Ten generate insufficient information on your skills and interests to formulate your job objective. If you use such services, make sure you are given one or both of the two most popular and reliable tests: *Myers-Briggs Type Indicator* and the *Strong-Campbell Interest Inventory*. You should find both tests helpful in better understanding your interests and decision-making styles. However, try our exercises before you hire a psychologist or visit a testing center. If you first complete these exercises, you will be in a better position to know exactly what you need from such centers. In many cases the career office at your local community college or women's center can administer these tests at minimum cost.

9. Job fairs or career conferences:

Job fairs or career conferences are organized by employment agencies to link applicants to employers. Usually consisting of one to two-day meetings in a hotel, employers meet with applicants as a group and on a one-to-one basis. Employers give presentations on their companies, resumes are circulated, and candidates are interviewed. Many of these conferences are organized to attract

hard-to-recruit groups, such as engineers, computer programmers, and clerical and service workers. These are
excellent sources for job leads and information—if you get
invited to the meeting or they are open to the public. Employers pay for this service—not applicants.

10. Professional associations:

Professional associations often provide placement assistance.
This usually consists of listing job vacancies and organizing
a job information exchange at annual conferences. These
meetings are good sources for making job contacts in
different geographic locations within a particular professional field. But don't expect too much. Talking to people (networking) at professional conferences will probably yield
better results than reading job listings and interviewing at
conference placement centers.

CHOOSE THE BEST

Other types of career planning and employment services are
growing and specializing in particular occupational fields. You may
wish to use these services as a supplement to this book.

Whatever you do, proceed with caution, know exactly what you
are getting into, and choose the best. Remember, there is no such
thing as a free lunch, and you often get less than what you pay for.
At the same time, the most expensive services are not necessarily the
best ones. Indeed, the free and inexpensive career planning services
offered by many community colleges—libraries, computerized career
assessment programs, testing, and workshops—are often much
superior to the other alternative services which can be expensive.
After reading this book, you should be able to make intelligent
decisions about what, when, where, and with what results you can use
professional assistance. Shop around, compare services and costs, ask
questions, talk to former clients, and read the fine print with your
lawyer before giving an employment expert a job using your hard
earned money!

Chapter Six

ALTERNATIVE CHOICES AND THE RIGHT "FIT"

Approaches to self-assessment are numerous and confusing. Everyone seems to offer their own unique theory, approach, test, or exercise purporting to provide insights into one's interests, values, skills, and abilities. For the uninitiated, this can be a bewildering experience as they attempt to acquire the most useful knowledge for directing their job search. Like the blind man feeling the trunk of an elephant, they're not sure what they have encountered. It could be an animal, but it might also be a tree.

Let's try to sort out the confusion by developing a clear idea of what we are doing and where we are going by addressing the key issues and questions involved in self-assessment. In so doing, you should be in a better position to determine which approaches will be most useful for your purposes.

ALTERNATIVE APPROACHES

You'll find numerous approaches to self-assessment. Some writers and career counselors claim you can do-it-on-your-own without the assistance of a professional. Indeed, some claim their self-directed exercises are just as valid as the testing instruments used by the professionals. Some claim they may even be superior to psychological testing. All you need to do is set aside a few hours of your time, complete the pencil and paper exercises, and analyze the information in reference to your particular job and career needs.

Your basic criteria for accepting an approach must be faith, common sense, and costs.

While we have no way of knowing how valid the self-directed approach is in comparison to many validated testing instruments, the self-directed approach does claim testimonials from thousands of people who claim it worked for them. When considering whether to use a self-directed versus a testing approach to self-assessment, your basic criteria for accepting an approach must be faith, common sense, and costs. In other words, is it worth your time and effort to engage in these exercises? If it sounds and feels good and others say it works, try it out; they won't hurt you. Self-directed approaches will only cost you time. If you spend the necessary time to complete the exercises, chances are you will gain a great deal of useful information on yourself for directing your job search. And you may join thousands of others with a testimonial that the exercises really worked for you. Most job and career books that include a self-assessment section use some variety of this self-directed approach. One of the most intensive and elaborate such exercises is Richard Bolles' *New Quick Job Hunting Map* (Ten Speed Press). We will have more to say later about this and other self-directed exercises.

But not all self-directed approaches are the same. Some are simple listings or checklists of information about your feelings, ideas, relationships, or decision-making style. For example, identify the 10 things you most like about your job. Or prioritize from a list of 100 work values the 10 that best describe what's important to you. Others are more elaborate self-graded tests such as our careering competencies exercise in Chapter Three. And still others are complicated and extremely time consuming exercises that integrate facts and values into a system that analyzes several aspects of your job and career experiences. We'll share one of the most popular and useful such exercises with you in Chapter Nine when we integrate the simpler exercises of Chapters Seven and Eight into constructing a comprehensive picture of your major strengths.

Underlying every approach is an implicit theory or set of assumptions about how you behave.

BEWARE OF UNDERLYING ASSUMPTIONS

You should also be aware that underlying every approach is an implicit theory or set of assumptions about how you behave. When related to issues about your future, each approach may generate certain advice on how you should relate to the world of work.

The major theory underlying the most popular self-directed exercises is a combination of **historical determinism** and **probability**: your future behavior will largely be a reflection of your past patterns of behavior. The emphasis here is on **patterns of behavior**. In the most sophisticated and sectarian form, these approaches direct you to identify your past patterns of motivated abilities and skills and then find jobs that will provide the best "fit" for your pattern. In the most extreme form, you will be told that you can't really do much about your patterns of behavior. They have been with you for years, and they will continue to dominate your behavior in the future. As this approach moves from description and explanation to prescription, it provides some sobering advice to those who believe in the power of self-transformation. Rather than try to change those patterns—which you probably can't or won't do anyway—it's best that you become more aware of them and learn to better live with yourself by seeking jobs and career opportunities that best use your "strengths."

Not a bad theory for most people who are generally pleased to learn that they indeed have these patterns of motivated abilities and skills. Indeed, many people are elated to literally rediscover themselves after having completed exercises based on this theory. However, others are less enthusiastic after they learn the approaches largely generate information they already know about themselves.

Knowing your strengths is interesting descriptive and explanatory information about you, but it doesn't provide much prescriptive content for directing your future.

Knowing your strengths is interesting descriptive and explanatory information about you, but it doesn't provide much prescriptive content for directing your future. For example, should you acquire new skills? What other jobs might be best suited for you? If you want to substantially increase your income, what should you do beyond what you have been doing in the past? Unfortunately, these self-directed exercises give you little guidance about your future since they are based upon historical information about you.

When proponents of this approach attempt to address questions about the future, they get themselves in a real quagmire by dispensing questionable advice. The advice is usually the same and is part of the theory underlying the approach: follow your patterns. This is very conservative and unenlightening advice that is sometimes further justified with reference to a conservative religious prescription—since God has established your pattern, you should learn to live with it and do the best you can within what are now your obvious limitations. There is little or no room in this approach for such notions as self-transformation—breaking out of one's past patterns to embark on a new future.

The clearest statements of this historical deterministic and probabilistic approach to self-assessment are found in *The Truth About You*, *What Color Is Your Parachute*, and *Where Do I Go From Here With My Life!* The approach is also implicit in the structure of *The Quick Job Hunting Map*. It is also found in a host of other literature and self-directed exercises associated with the works of Haldane, Holland, Bolles, Crystal, and their followers. With certain qualifications and revisions, this approach also occupies a major place in this book.

This is not to say these self-directed approaches do not work or are inherently deficient. Rather, they work well for thousands of people who embrace them and are willing to plan their futures around the notion of a pattern of motivated abilities and skills. Indeed, for 85 percent of the population, such an approach is very appropriate. They are not interested in self-transformation—just get a better handle on their strengths and direct their lives accordingly.

Our point is this: like any approach, these approaches have limitations. They can only take you so far, depending on what you want to do with your life. If you already know your strengths but want to acquire new strengths that will take you into new job and career directions, you'll simply have to use other approaches that are less historical and more future in orientation. The most important approaches will deal with issues of change and self-transformation.

For 85 percent of the population,
the self-directed approach is
very appropriate.

A JOB-TARGETED APPROACH

Another problem with many self-assessment approaches is that they help you generate self-understanding about your past interests, values, abilities, and skills, but they don't go to the next important step—linking that self-knowledge to specific jobs and careers most appropriate for your particular mix of skills or pattern of motivated abilities and skills. Indeed many people already know what they do well and enjoy doing, but they want to know what alternative jobs and careers are the most likely candidates for their experience. Many teachers, for example, know they have strong organization, communication, and supervision skills, but they don't know what types of jobs outside teaching might offer them better career opportunities, especially in terms of salaries and advancement. Many of the best jobs for the 1990s outlined in Chapter Two, for example, may be appropriate for your particular mix of motivated skills and abilities.

Our approach to self-assessment incorporates many of the previous approaches and then targets the self-assessment information toward alternative jobs and careers. In other words, you first need to know about your strengths through self-assessment and then relate those strengths to special jobs:

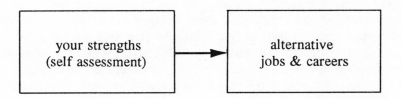

Once you know what jobs are likely to be the best "fit" for your particular mix of strengths, you will be well on the road to targeting your other job search activities (resumes, letters, networking, interviews) toward specific organizations, employers, and jobs.

ASK THE RIGHT QUESTIONS

We know that as much as 70 percent of the solution to most problems is found in first asking the right questions. In fact, you can easily reduce the complexity and confusion surrounding the many self-assessment approaches by focusing your attention on two basic questions:

1. What do you do well?

2. What do you enjoy doing?

The first question addresses your **skills and abilities**. The second question helps identify your **interests, values, and motivations**. Once you've answered these questions, you next need to link your skills and abilities (Question 1) with your interests, values, and motivations

(Question 2). When integrated with each other, these elements become your **motivated abilities and skills (MAS)**. When examined through a series of self-assessment exercises, they become identified as your **pattern** of motivated abilities and skills (MAS pattern). This pattern becomes your unique set of job and career **strengths** that are best used in particular types of jobs.

What you ultimately need to do is find the best "fit" between your strengths (MAS pattern) and alternative jobs. You do this by first learning what your strengths are (self-assessment centered on identifying your MAS pattern) and then aligning them with different jobs that seem conducive to your strengths.

Put another way, this process involves five distinct yet closely related steps in the process of discovering the best jobs for you. These steps are outlined on page 73. A sixth step would involve restating your general job and career objective (Step 4) at a more specific level for the jobs you seek. This objective would appear on your resume. It would also be the focus for your networking activities as well as a subject to be elaborated upon during job interviews.

The remaining chapters examine each of these steps in the process of discovering the right job for you. In addition, we return to the issue of historical determinism versus self-transformation in Chapter Ten when we examine alternative approaches to self-assessment.

FIND THE BEST JOBS PROCESS

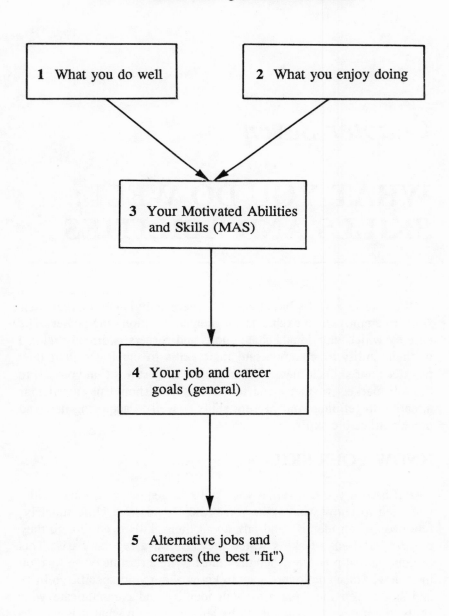

Chapter Seven

WHAT YOU DO WELL: SKILLS AND ABILITIES

We live in a skills-based society where individuals market their skills to employers in exchange for money, position, and power. The ease by which individuals change jobs and careers is directly related to their ability to communicate their skills to employers and then transfer their skills to new work settings. To best position yourself in the job markets of today and tomorrow, you should pay particular attention to refining your present skills as well as acquiring new and more marketable skills.

KNOW YOUR SKILLS

But before you can refine your skills or acquire additional skills, you need to know what skills you presently possess. Unfortunately, few people can identify and talk about their skills even though they possess hundreds of skills which they use on a regular basis. This becomes a real problem when they must write a resume or go to a job interview. Since employers want to know about your specific abilities and skills, you must learn to both identify and communicate your skills to employers. You should be able to explain what it is you do well and give examples relevant to employers' needs.

What skills do you already have to offer employers? If you have just completed an educational program relevant to today's job market, the skills you have to offer are most likely related to the subject matter you studied. If you are changing jobs or careers, the skills you wish to communicate to employers will be those things you already have demonstrated you can do in specific jobs. They are your demonstrated abilities to accomplish work specific tasks.

TYPES OF SKILLS

Most people possess two types of skills that define their accomplishments and strengths as well as enable them to enter and advance within the job market:

- work-content skills

- functional skills

You need to acquaint yourself with these skills before communicating them to employers.

We assume you have already acquired certain **work-content skills** necessary to function effectively in today's job market. These "hard skills" are easy to recognize since they are often identified as "qualifications" for specific jobs; they are the subject of most educational and training programs. Work-content skills tend to be technical and job-specific in nature. Examples of such skills include proficiency in typing, programming computers, repairing air conditioners, or operating an X-ray machine. They may require formal training, are associated with specific trades or professions, are used only in certain job and career settings, and use a separate skills vocabulary, jargon, and subject matter for specifying technical qualifications for individuals entering and advancing in an occupation. While these skills do not transfer well from one occupation to another, they are critical for entering and advancing within certain occupations.

At the same time, you possess numerous **functional/transferable skills** employers readily seek along with your work-content skills. These "soft skills" are associated with numerous job settings, are mainly acquired through experience rather than formal training, and can be communicated through a general vocabulary. Functional/transferable skills are less easy to recognize since they tend to be linked to **dealing with processes** (communicating, problem-solving, motivating) rather than **doing things** (programming a computer, building a house, repairing air conditioners). While most people have only a few work-content skills, they have numerous—perhaps as many as 300—functional/transferable skills. These skills enable job seekers to more easily change jobs. But you must first be aware of your functional skills before you can adequately relate them to the job market.

Most people view the world of work in traditional occupational job skill terms. This is a **structural view** of occupational realities. Occupational fields are seen as consisting of separate and distinct jobs which, in turn, require specific work-content skills. From this perspective, occupations and jobs are relatively self-contained entities. Social work, for example, is seen as being different from paralegal work; social workers, therefore, are not "qualified" to seek paralegal work.

Functional skills can be transferred from one job or career to another.

On the other hand, a **functional view** of occupations and jobs emphasizes similar characteristics among jobs as well as common linkages between different occupations. Although the structure of occupations and jobs may differ, they have similar functions. They involve working with people, data, processes, and objects. If you work with people, data, processes, and objects in one occupation, you can transfer that experience to other occupations which have similar functions. Once you understand how your skills relate to the functions as well as investigate the structure of different occupations, you should be prepared to make job changes from one occupational field to another. Whether you possess the necessary work-content skills to qualify for entry into the other occupational field is another question altogether.

The skills we identify and help you organize in this chapter are the functional skills career counselors normally emphasize when advising clients to assess their **strengths**. In contrast to work-content skills, functional skills can be transferred from one job or career to another. They enable individuals to make some job and career changes without the need to acquire additional education and training. They constitute an important bridge for moving from one occupation to another.

Before you decide if you need more education or training, you should first assess both your functional and work-content skills to see how they can be transferred to other jobs and occupations. Once you do this, you should be better prepared to communicate your qualifications to employers with a rich skills-based vocabulary.

YOUR STRENGTHS

Regardless of what combination of work-content and functional skills you possess, a job search must begin with identifying your strengths. Without knowing these, your job search will lack content and focus. After all, your goal should be to find a job that is fit for you rather than one you think you might be able to fit into. Of course, you also want to find a job for which there is a demand, such as those identified in Chapter Two. This particular focus requires a well-defined approach to identifying and communicating your skills to others. You can best do this by asking the right questions about your strengths and then conducting a systematic self-assessment of what you do best.

ASK THE RIGHT QUESTIONS

Knowing the right questions to ask will save you time and steer you into productive job search channels from the very beginning. Asking the wrong questions can cripple your job search efforts and leave you frustrated. The questions must be understood from the perspectives of both employers and applicants.

Two of the most humbling questions you will encounter in your job search are

"Why should I hire you?"

"What are your weaknesses?"

While employers may not directly ask these questions, feel assured they are asking them nonetheless. If these questions are not answered in a positive manner—directly, indirectly, verbally, or nonverbally— your job search will likely founder and you will join the ranks of the unsuccessful and disillusioned job searchers who feel something is wrong with them. Individuals who have lost their jobs are particularly vulnerable to these questions since many have lowered self-esteem and self-image as a result of the job loss. Many such people focus on what is wrong rather than what is right about themselves. Such thinking creates self-fulfilling prophecies and is self-destructive in the job market. By all means avoid such negative thinking.

> ## *Employers want to hire your value or strengths—not your weaknesses.*

Employers want to hire your **value or strengths**—not your weaknesses. Since it is easier to identify and interpret weaknesses, employers look for indicators of your strengths by trying to identify your weaknesses. Your job is to communicate your strengths to employers. The more successful you are in doing this, the better off you will be in relation to both employers and fellow applicants.

Unfortunately, many people work against their own best interests. Not knowing their strengths, they market their weaknesses by first identifying job vacancies and then trying to fit their "qualifications" into job descriptions. This approach often frustrates applicants; it presents a picture of a job market which is not interested in the applicant's strengths. This leads some people toward acquiring new skills which they hope will be marketable, even though they do not enjoy using them. Millions of individuals find themselves in such misplaced situations. Your task is to avoid joining the ranks of the misplaced and unhappy work force by first understanding your skills and then relating them to your interests and goals. In so doing, you will be in a better position to target your job search toward jobs that should become especially rewarding and fulfilling.

FUNCTIONAL/TRANSFERABLE SKILLS

We know most people stumble into jobs by accident. Some are at the right place at the right time to take advantage of a job or career opportunity. Others work hard at trying to fit into jobs listed in classified ads, employment agencies, and personnel offices; identified through friends and acquaintances; or found by knocking on doors. After 15 to 20 years in the work world, many people wish they had better planned their careers from the very start. All of a sudden they are unhappily locked into jobs because of retirement benefits and the family responsibilities of raising children and meeting monthly mortgage payments.

After 10 or 20 years of work experience, most people have a good idea of what they don't like to do. While their values are more set than when they first began working, many people are still unclear as to what they do well and how their skills fit into the job market. What other jobs, for example, might they be qualified to perform? If they have the opportunity to change jobs or careers—either voluntarily or forced through termination—and find the time to plan the change, they can move into jobs and careers which fit their skills.

The key to understanding your non-technical strengths is to identify your transferable or functional skills. Once you have done this, you will be better prepared to identify what it is you want to do. Moreover, your self-image and self-esteem will improve. Better still, you will be prepared to communicate your strengths to others through a rich skills-based vocabulary. These outcomes are critically important for writing your resume and letters as well as for conducting informational and job interviews.

Let's illustrate the concept of functional/transferable skills by examining the case of educators. Many educators view their skills in strict work-content terms—knowledge of a particular subject matter such as math, history, English, physics, or music. When looking outside education for employment, many educators seek jobs which will use their subject matter skills. However, they soon discover that non-educational institutions are not a ready market for such "skills."

On the other hand, educators possess many other skills that are directly transferable to business and industry. Most educators are not aware of these skills and thus they fail to communicate their strengths to others. For example, research shows that graduate students in the humanities most frequently possess these transferable skills, in order of importance:

critical thinking	general knowledge
research techniques	cultural perspective
perseverance	teaching ability
self-discipline	self-confidence
insight	imagination
writing	leadership ability

Most functional/transferable skills can be classified into two general skills and trait categories—organizational/interpersonal skills and personality/work-style traits. Each category is defined by numerous distinct skills:

Organizational and Interpersonal Skills

___ communicating	___ trouble shooting
___ problem solving	___ implementing
___ analyzing/assessing	___ self-understanding
___ planning	___ understanding
___ decision-making	___ setting goals
___ innovating	___ conceptualizing
___ thinking logically	___ generalizing
___ evaluating	___ managing time
___ identifying problems	___ creating
___ synthesizing	___ judging
___ forecasting	___ controlling
___ tolerating ambiguity	___ organizing
___ motivating	___ persuading
___ leading	___ encouraging
___ selling	___ improving
___ performing	___ designing
___ reviewing	___ consulting
___ attaining	___ teaching
___ team building	___ cultivating
___ updating	___ advising
___ coaching	___ training
___ supervising	___ interpreting
___ estimating	___ achieving

___ negotiating   ___ reporting
___ administering ___ managing

Personality and Work-Style Traits

___ diligent   ___ honest
___ patient   ___ reliable
___ innovative   ___ perceptive
___ persistent   ___ assertive
___ tactful   ___ sensitive
___ loyal   ___ astute
___ successful   ___ risk taker
___ versatile   ___ easy going
___ enthusiastic   ___ calm
___ out-going   ___ flexible
___ expressive   ___ competent
___ adaptable   ___ punctual
___ democratic   ___ receptive
___ resourceful   ___ diplomatic
___ determining   ___ self-confident
___ creative   ___ tenacious
___ open   ___ discrete
___ objective   ___ talented
___ warm   ___ empathic
___ orderly   ___ tidy
___ tolerant   ___ candid
___ frank   ___ adventuresome
___ cooperative   ___ firm
___ dynamic   ___ sincere
___ self-starter   ___ initiator
___ precise   ___ competent
___ sophisticated ___ diplomatic
___ effective   ___ efficient

Use the following exercises to identify both your work-content and transferable skills. These self-assessment techniques stress your positives or strengths rather than identify your negatives or weaknesses. They should generate a rich vocabulary for communicating your "qualifications" to employers. Each exercise requires different investments of your time and effort as well as varying degrees of assistance from other people.

If you feel these exercises are inadequate for your needs, by all means seek professional assistance from a testing or assessment center staffed by a licensed psychologist. These centers do in-depth testing which goes further than these self-directed skill exercises.

CHECKLIST METHOD

This is the simplest method for identifying your strengths. Review the two types of transferable skills outlined on pages 80-81. Place a "1" in front of the skills that **strongly** characterize you; assign a "2" to those skills that describe you to a **large extent**; put a "3" before those that describe you to **some extent**. After completing this exercise, review the lists and rank order the 10 characteristics that best describe you on each list.

SKILLS MAP

Richard N. Bolles has produced two well-known exercises for identifying transferable skills based upon John Holland's typology of work environments. In his book, *The Three Boxes of Life* (Ten Speed Press), he develops a checklist of 100 transferable skills. They are organized into 12 categories or types of skills: using hands, body, words, senses, numbers, intuition, analytical thinking, creativity, helpfulness, artistic abilities, leadership, and follow-through.

Bolles' second exercise, *"The Quick Job Hunting Map,"* expands upon this first one. The *"Map"* is a checklist of 222 skills. This exercise requires you to identify seven of your most satisfying accomplishments, achievements, jobs, or roles. After writing a page about each experience, you relate each to the checklist of 222 skills. The *"Map"* should give you a comprehensive picture of what skills you (1) use most frequently, and (2) enjoy using in satisfying and successful settings. While this exercise may take six hours to complete, it yields an enormous amount of data on past strengths. Furthermore, the *"Map"* generates a rich skills vocabulary for communicating your strengths to others. The *"Map"* is found in the appendix of Bolles' *What Color Is Your Parachute?* (Ten Speed Press) or it can be purchased separately in beginning, advanced, or "new" versions from Ten Speed Press. His books as well as the latest version (1990) of his popular *New Quick Job Hunting Map* can be ordered directly from Impact Publications by completing the order information at the end of this book.

AUTOBIOGRAPHY OF ACCOMPLISHMENTS

Write a lengthy essay about your life accomplishments. This could range from 20 to 100 pages. After completing the essay, go through it page by page to identify what you most enjoyed doing (working with different kinds of information, people, and things) and what skills you used most frequently as well as enjoyed using. Finally, identify those skills you wish to continue using. After analyzing and synthesizing this data, you should have a relatively clear picture of your strongest skills.

COMPUTERIZED SKILLS ASSESSMENT SYSTEMS

While the previous self-directed exercises required you to either respond to checklists of skills or reconstruct and analyze your past job experiences, several computerized self-assessment programs are designed to help individuals identify their skills. Many of the programs are available in schools, colleges, and libraries. Some of the most widely used programs include:

- *Discover II*
- *Sigi-Plus*
- *Computerized Career Assessment and Planning Program*

These comprehensive career planning programs do much more than assess skills. As we will see in Chapter Nine, they also integrate other key components in the career planning process—interests, goals, related jobs, college majors, education and training programs, and job search plans. These programs are widely available in schools, colleges, and libraries across the country. You might check with the career or counseling center at your local community college to see what computerized career assessment systems are available for your use. They are relatively easy to use and they generate a great deal of useful career planning information.

Chapter Eight

WHAT YOU ENJOY DOING: INTERESTS AND VALUES

Knowing what you do well is essential to understanding your strengths. However, knowing your abilities and skills alone does not necessarily give your job search the direction it needs for finding your best job. You also need to know your work values and interests. These provide the basis for setting goals and motivating you to target your skills into certain job and career directions. The individual who types 120 words a minute, for example, possesses an excellent and highly marketable skill. But if the person doesn't enjoy using this skill and is more interested in working outdoors, this typing skill does not become a motivated skill nor is the individual likely to pursue a typing job. Your interests and values will determine whether or not certain skills should play a central role in your job search.

WORK INTERESTS

We all have interests. Some are related to jobs and careers whereas others relate to activities that define our hobbies and leisure activities. According to the *Guide For Occupational Exploration*, all jobs in the United States can be classified into 12 interest areas. Examine the following list of interest areas. In the first column check those work areas that appeal to you. In the second column rank order those areas you checked in the first column. Start with "1" to indicate the most interesting:

YOUR WORK INTERESTS

Yes/No (x)	Ranking (1-12)	Interest Area
____	____	**Artistic:** an interest in creative expression of feelings or ideas.
____	____	**Scientific:** an interest in discovering, collecting, and analyzing information about the natural world, and in applying scientific research findings to problems in medicine, the life sciences, and the nature sciences.
____	____	**Plants and animals:** an interest in working with plants and animals, usually outdoors.
____	____	**Protective:** an interest in using authority to protect people and property.
____	____	**Mechanical:** an interest in applying mechanical principles to practical situations by using machines or hand tools.
____	____	**Industrial:** an interest in repetitive, concrete, organized activities done in a factory setting.
____	____	**Business detail:** an interest in organized, clearly defined activities requiring accuracy and attention to details, primarily in an office setting.

____   ____   **Selling:** an interest in bringing others to a particular point of view by using personal persuasion as well as sales and promotion techniques.

____   ____   **Accommodating:** an interest in catering to the wishes and needs of others, usually on a one-to-one basis.

____   ____   **Humanitarian:** an interest in helping others with their mental, spiritual, social, physical, or vocational needs.

____   ____   **Leading and influencing:** an interest in leading and influencing others by using high-level verbal or numerical abilities.

____   ____   **Physical performing:** an interest in physical activities performed before an audience.

The *Guide For Occupational Exploration* also includes other checklists relating to home-based and leisure activities that may or may not relate to your work interests. If you are unclear about your work interests, you might want to consult these other interest exercises. You may discover that some of your home-based and leisure activity interests should become your work interests. Examples of such interests include:

LEISURE AND HOME-BASED INTERESTS

____   Acting in a play or amateur variety show.

____   Advising family members on their personal problems.

____   Announcing or emceeing a program.

____   Applying first aid in emergencies as a volunteer.

____   Building model airplanes, automobiles, or boats.

___ Building or repairing radio or television sets.

___ Buying large quantities of food or other products for an organization.

___ Campaigning for political candidates or issues.

___ Canning and preserving food.

___ Carving small wooden objects.

___ Coaching children or youth in sports activities.

___ Collecting experiments involving plants.

___ Conducting house-to-house or telephone surveys for a PTA or other organization.

___ Creating or styling hairdos for friends.

___ Designing your own greeting cards and writing original verses.

___ Developing film.

___ Doing impersonations.

___ Doing public speaking or debating.

___ Entertaining at parties or other events.

___ Helping conduct physical exercises for disabled people.

___ Making ceramic objects.

___ Modeling clothes for a fashion show.

___ Mounting and framing pictures.

___ Nursing sick pets.

____ Painting the interior or exterior of a home.

____ Playing a musical instrument.

____ Refinishing or re-upholstering furniture.

____ Repairing electrical household appliances.

____ Repairing the family car.

____ Repairing or assembling bicycles.

____ Repairing plumbing in the house.

____ Speaking on radio or television.

____ Taking photographs.

____ Teaching in Sunday School.

____ Tutoring pupils in school subjects.

____ Weaving rugs or making quilts.

____ Writing articles, stories, or plays.

____ Writing songs for club socials or amateur plays.

Indeed, many people turn hobbies or home activities into full-time jobs after deciding that such "work" is what they really enjoy doing.

Other popular exercises designed to identify your work interests include John Holland's *"The Self-Directed Search"* which is found in his book, ***Making Vocational Choices: A Theory of Careers***. It is also published as a separate testing instrument, ***The Self-Directed Search—a Guide to Educational and Vocational Planning***. Developed from Holland's Vocational Preference Inventory, this popular self-administered, self-scored, and self-interpreted inventory helps individuals quickly identify what type of work environment they are motivated to seek—realistic, investigative, artistic, social, enterprising, or conventional—and aligns these work environments with lists of common occupational titles. An easy exercise to use, it gives you a quick overview of your orientation toward different types of work settings that interest you.

Holland's self-directed search is also the basic framework used in developing Bolles' *"The Quick Job Hunting Map"* as found in his **What Color Is Your Parachute?** and *The New Quick Job Hunting Map* books.

For more sophisticated treatments of work interests, which are also validated through testing procedures, contact a career counselor, women's center, or testing and assessment center for information on the following tests:

- Strong-Campbell Interest Inventory
- Myers-Briggs Type Indicator
- Edwards Personal Preference Schedule
- Kuder Occupational Interest Survey
- APTICOM
- Jackson Vocational Interest Survey
- Ramak Inventory
- Vocational Interest Inventory
- Career Assessment Inventory
- Temperament and Values Inventory

Numerous other job and career interest inventories are also available. For further information, contact a career counselor or consult Educational Testing Service which compiles such tests. *The ETS Test Collection Catalog* (New York: Oryx Press), which is available in many library reference sections, lists most of these tests. The *Mental Measurements Yearbook* (Lincoln, NE: University of Nebraska Press) also surveys many of the major testing and assessment instruments.

Keep in mind that not all testing and assessment instruments used by career counselors are equally valid for career planning purposes. While the Strong-Campbell Interest Inventory appears to be the most relevant for career decision-making, the Myers-Briggs Type Indicator has become extremely popular during the past five years. It is most useful for measuring individual personality and decision-making styles than for predicting career choices. It is most widely used in pastoral counseling, student personnel, and business and religious organizations for measuring personality and decision-making styles. How these elements relate to career choices remains uncertain. In the meantime, many career counselors find Holland's *The Self-Directed Search* an excellent self-directed alternative to these professionally administered and interpreted tests.

WORK VALUES

Work values are those things you like to do. They give you pleasure and enjoyment. Most jobs involve a combination of likes and dislikes. By identifying what you both like and dislike about jobs, you should be able to better identify jobs that involve tasks that you will most enjoy.

Several exercises can help you identify your work values. First, identify what most satisfies you about work by completing the following exercise:

MY WORK VALUES

I prefer employment which enables me to:

____ contribute to society	____ be creative
____ have contact with people	____ supervise others
____ work alone	____ work with details
____ work with a team	____ gain recognition
____ compete with others	____ acquire security
____ make decisions	____ make a lot of money
____ work under pressure	____ help others
____ use power and authority	____ solve problems
____ acquire new knowledge	____ take risks
____ be a recognized expert	____ work at my own pace

Select four work values from the above list which are the most important to you and list them in the space below. List any other work values (desired satisfactions) which were not listed above but are nonetheless important to you:

1. _____

2. _____

3. _____

4. _____

Another approach to identifying work values is outlined in the *Guide For Occupational Exploration.* If you feel you need to go beyond the above exercises, try this one. In the first column check those values that are most important to you. In the second column rank order the five most important values:

RANKING WORK VALUES

Yes/No (x)	Ranking (1-5)	Work Values
_____	_____	**Adventure:** Working in a job that requires taking risks.
_____	_____	**Authority:** Working in a job in which you use your position to control others.
_____	_____	**Competition:** Working in a job in which you compete with others.
_____	_____	**Creativity and self-expression:** Working in a job in which you use your imagination to find new ways to do or say something.

_____ _____ **Flexible work schedule:** Working in a job in which you choose your hours to work.

_____ _____ **Helping others:** Working in a job in which you provide direct services to persons with problems.

_____ _____ **High salary:** Working in a job where many workers earn a large amount of money.

_____ _____ **Independence:** Working in a job in which you decide for yourself what work to do and how to do it.

_____ _____ **Influencing others:** Working in a job in which you influence the opinions of others or decisions of others.

_____ _____ **Intellectual stimulation:** Working in a job which requires a great amount of thought and reasoning.

_____ _____ **Leadership:** Working in a job which you direct, manage, or supervise the activities of others.

_____ _____ **Outside work:** Working out-of-doors.

_____ _____ **Persuading:** Working in a job in which you personally convince others to take certain actions.

_____ _____ **Physical work:** Working in a job which requires substantial physical activity.

_____ _____ **Prestige:** Working in a job which gives you status and respect in the community.

_____ _____ **Public attention:** Working in a job in which you attract immediate notice because of appearance or activity.

_____ _____ **Public contact:** Working in a job in which you have day-to-day dealings with the public.

_____ _____ **Recognition:** Working in a job in which you gain public notice.

_____ _____ **Research work:** Working in a job in which you search for and discover new facts and develop ways to apply them.

_____ _____ **Routine work:** Working in a job in which you follow established procedures requiring little change.

_____ _____ **Seasonal work:** Working in a job in which you are employed only at certain times of the year.

_____ _____ **Travel:** Working in a job in which you take frequent trips.

_____ _____ **Variety:** Working in a job in which your duties change frequently.

_____ _____ **Work with children:** Working in a job in which you teach or otherwise care for children.

_____ _____ **Work with hands:** Working in a job in which you use your hands or hand tools.

_____ _____ **Work with machines or equipment:** Working in a job in which you use machines or equipment.

_____   _____   **Work with numbers:** Working in a job
in which you use mathematics or statistics.

Second, develop a comprehensive list of your past and present **job frustrations and dissatisfactions**. This should help you identify negative factors you should avoid in future jobs.

MY JOB FRUSTRATIONS
AND DISSATISFACTIONS

List as well as rank order as many past and present things that frustrate or make you dissatisfied and unhappy in job situations:

Rank

1. _____   _____

2. _____   _____

3. _____   _____

4. _____   _____

5. _____   _____

6. _____   _____

7. _____   _____

8. _____   _____

9. _____   _____

10. _____   _____

Third, brainstorm a list of *"Ten or More Things I Love to Do."* Identify which ones could be incorporated into what kinds of work environments:

TEN OR MORE THINGS I LOVE TO DO

Item	Related Environment

1. _____   _____

2. _____   _____

3. _____   _____

4. _____   _____

5. _____   _____

6. _____   _____

7. _____   _____

8. _____   _____

9. _____   _____

10. _____   _____

Fourth, list at least ten things you most enjoy about work and rank each item accordingly:

TEN THINGS I ENJOY THE MOST
ABOUT WORK

Rank

1. _____   _____

2. _____   _____

3. _____   _____

4. _____   _____

5. _____   _____

6. _____   _____

7. _____   _____

8. _____   _____

9. _____   _____

10. _____   _____

Fifth, you should also identify the types of interpersonal environments you prefer working in. Do this by specifying the types of people you like and dislike associating with:

INTERPERSONAL ENVIRONMENTS

Characteristics of people I like working with:	Characteristics of people I dislike working with:
_____	_____
_____	_____
_____	_____
_____	_____
_____	_____
_____	_____
_____	_____
_____	_____

COMPUTERIZED SYSTEMS

Several computerized self-assessment programs are available that largely focus on career interests and values. The two major systems, *Discover II* and *Sigi-Plus*, include career interest segments. Some other popular systems are:

- *Career Interest Program*
- *Computerized Career Assessment and Planning Program*
- *Computerized Career Information System*
- *Values Auction Deluxe*

You should be able to get access to some of these and other related computer programs through your local community college, career center, or library.

YOUR FUTURE AS OBJECTIVES

All of these exercises are designed to explore your past and present work-related values. At the same time, you need to project your values into the **future**. What, for example, do you want to do over the next 10 to 20 years? We'll return to this type of value question when we address the critical objective setting stage of the job search process in Chapter Eleven.

Chapter Nine

IDENTIFY YOUR MOTIVATED ABILITIES AND SKILLS (MAS)

Once you know what you do well and enjoy doing, you next need to analyze those interests, values, abilities, and skills that form your **recurring motivated pattern**. This pattern is the single most important piece of information you need to know about yourself in the whole self-assessment process. If you only know your skills and abilities—without realizing how they directly relate to your interests and values—you will lack a critical piece of information you need for directing your job search toward discovering the best job for you.

WHAT'S YOUR MAS?

The concept of **motivated abilities and skills (MAS)** enables us to relate your interests and values to your skills and abilities. But how do we identify your MAS beyond the questions and exercises we've outlined thus far?

Your pattern of motivated abilities and skills becomes evident once you analyze your **achievements or accomplishments**. For it is your achievements that tell us what you both did well and enjoyed doing. If we analyze and synthesize many of your achievements, we are likely to identify a recurring pattern that most likely goes back to your childhood and which will continue to characterize your achievements in the future.

Numerous self-directed exercises can assist you in identifying your pattern of motivated abilities and skills. The basic requirements for making these exercises work for you are time and analytical ability. You must spend a great deal of **time** detailing your achievements by looking at your past history of accomplishments. Once you have completed the historical reconstruction task, you must comb through your "stories" to identify recurring themes and patterns. This requires a high level of **analytical ability** which you may or may not possess. If analysis and synthesis are not two of your strong skills, you may need to seek assistance from a friend or professional who is good at analyzing and synthesizing information presented in narrative form. Career counseling firms such as Haldane Associates and People Management, Inc. are known for their use of this type of motivated pattern approach; they should be able to assist you.

Several paper and pencil exercises are designed to help identify your pattern of motivated abilities and skills. In the remainder of this chapter we outline some of the most popular and thorough such exercises that have proved useful to thousands of people.

THE SKILLS MAP

Richard Bolles' *"Quick Job Hunting Map"* has become a standard self-assessment tool for thousands of job seekers and career changers who are willing to spend the time and effort necessary for discovering their pattern of motivated abilities and skills. Offering a checklist of over 200 skills organized around John Holland's concept of *"The Self-Directed Search"* for defining work environments (realistic, investigative, artistic, social, enterprising, and conventional), the *"Map"* requires you to identify seven of your most satisfying accomplishments, achievements, jobs, or roles. After detailing each achievement, you analyze the details of each in relation to the checklist of skills. Once you do this for all seven achievements, you should generate a comprehensive picture of what skills you (1) use most frequently, and (2) enjoy using in satisfying and successful settings. This exercise not only yields an enormous amount of information on your interests, values, skills, and abilities, it also assists you in the process of analyzing the data. If done properly, the *"Map"* should also generate a rich *"Map"* vocabulary which you should use in your resumes and letters as well as in interviews.

The *"Map"* is available in different forms and for different levels of experience. The most popular versions are found in the Appendix of Bolles' **What Color Is Your Parachute?** and **The Three Boxes of Life** as well as in a separate publication entitled **The New Quick Job Hunting Map**. These three publications can be ordered directly from Impact Publications by completing the order information at the end of this book. The map is also available in three other versions: **The Beginning Quick Job-Hunting Map, How to Create a Picture of Your Ideal Job or Next Career**, and **The Classic Quick Job-Hunting Map**. These versions of the *"Map"* are most conveniently available directly from the publisher, Ten Speed Press (P.O. Box 7123, Berkeley, CA 94707).

We highly recommend using the *"Map"* because of the ease in which it can be used. If you will spend the six to twenty hours necessary to complete it properly, the *"Map"* will give you some important information about yourself. Unfortunately, many people become overwhelmed by the exercise and either decide not to complete it or they try to save time by not doing it according to the directions. You simply must follow the directions and spend the time and effort necessary if you want to get the maximum benefit from this exercise.

Keep in mind that like most self-assessment devices, there is nothing magical about the *"Map."* Its basic organizing principles are simple. Like other exercises designed to uncover your pattern of motivated abilities and skills, this one is based on a theory of historical determinism and probability. In other words, once you uncover your pattern, get prepared to acknowledge it and live with it in the future.

AUTOBIOGRAPHY OF ACCOMPLISHMENTS

Less structured than the *"Map"* device, the "Autobiography of Accomplishments" exercise requires you to write a lengthy essay about your life accomplishments. Your essay may run anywhere from 20 to 200 pages. After completing it, go through it page by page to identify what you most enjoyed doing (working with different kinds of data, people, processes, and objects) and what skills you used most frequently as well as enjoyed using. Finally, identify those skills you wish to continue using. After analyzing and synthesizing this data, you should have a relatively clear picture of your strongest skills.

This exercise requires a great deal of self-discipline and analytic skill. To do it properly, you must write as much as possible, and in as much detail as possible, about your accomplishments. The richer the detail, the better will be your analysis.

MOTIVATED SKILLS EXERCISE

Our final exercise, the Motivated Skills Exercise, is one of the most complex and time consuming self-assessment exercises. However, it yields some of the best data on motivated abilities and skills, and it is especially useful for those who feel they need a more thorough analysis of their past achievements. This device is widely used by career counselors. Initially developed by Haldane Associates, this particular exercise is variously referred to as *"Success Factor Analysis," "System to Identify Motivated Skills,"* or *"Intensive Skills Identification."*

This technique helps you identify which skills you **enjoy** using. While you can use this technique on your own, it is best to work with someone else. Since you will need six to eight hours to properly complete this exercise, divide your time into two or three work sessions.

The exercise consists of six steps. The steps follow the basic pattern of generating raw data, identifying patterns, analyzing the data through reduction techniques, and synthesizing the patterns into a transferable skills vocabulary. You need strong analytical skills to complete this exercise on your own. The six steps include:

1. **Identify 15-20 achievements:** These consist of things you enjoyed doing, believe you did well, and felt a sense of satisfaction, pride, or accomplishment in doing. You can see yourself performing at your best and enjoying your experiences when you analyze your achievements. This information reveals your motivations since it deals entirely with your voluntary behavior. In addition, it identifies what is right with you by focusing on your positives and strengths. Identify achievements throughout your life, beginning with your childhood. Your achievements should relate to specific experiences—not general

ones—and may be drawn from work, leisure, education, military, or home life. Put each achievement at the top of a separate sheet of paper. For example, your achievements might appear as follows:

SAMPLE ACHIEVEMENT STATEMENTS

"When I was 10 years old, I started a small paper route and built it up to the largest in my district."

"I started playing chess in ninth grade and earned the right to play first board on my high school chess team in my junior year."

"Learned to play the piano and often played for church services while in high school."

"Designed and constructed a dress for a 4-H demonstration project."

"Although I was small compared to other guys, I made the first string on my high school football team."

"I graduated from high school with honors even though I was very active in school clubs and had to work part-time."

"I was the first in my family to go to college and one of the few from my high school. Worked part-time and summers. A real struggle, but I made it."

"Earned an 'A' grade on my senior psychology project from a real tough professor."

"Finished my master's degree while working full-time and attending to my family responsibilities."

―――――――――――

"Proposed a chef's course for junior high boys. Got it approved. Developed it into a very popular elective."

―――――――――――

"Designed the plans for our house and had it constructed within budget."

2. Prioritize your seven most significant achievements.

YOUR MOST SIGNIFICANT ACHIEVEMENTS

1. _____

2. _____

3. _____

4. _____

5. _____

6. _____

7. _____

3. Write a full page on each of your prioritized achievements. You should describe:

- How you initially became involved.
- The details of **what you did** and **how you did it**.
- What was especially enjoyable or satisfying to you.

Use copies of the following form to outline your achievements.

DETAILING YOUR ACHIEVEMENTS

ACHIEVEMENT # __: _____

_____

1. How did I initially become involved? _____

_____

_____

_____

2. What did I do? _____

_____

_____

_____

_____

3. How did I do it? _____

_____

_____

_____

_____

4. What was especially enjoyable about doing it? _____

_____

_____

_____

_____

4. **Elaborate on your achievements:** Have one or two other people interview you. For each achievement have them note on a separate sheet of paper any terms used to reveal your skills, abilities, and personal qualities. To elaborate details, the interviewer(s) may ask:

   - What was involved in the achievement?
   - What was your part?
   - What did you actually do?
   - How did you go about that?

   Clarify any vague areas by providing an example or illustration of what you actually did. This interview should clarify the details of your activities by asking only "what" and "how" questions. Reproduce the *"Strength Identification Interview"* form at the end of this chapter (page 108) to guide you through this interview.

5. **Identify patterns by examining the interviewer's notes :** Together identify the recurring skills, abilities, and personal qualities **demonstrated** in your major achievements. Search for patterns. Your skills pattern should be clear at this point; you should feel comfortable with it. If you have questions, review the data. If you disagree with a conclusion, disregard it. The results must accurately and honestly reflect how you operate.

6. **Synthesize the information by clustering similar skills into categories:** For example, your skills might be grouped in the following manner:

Investigate/Survey/Read Inquire/Probe/Question	Teach/Train/Drill Perform/Show/Demonstrate
Learn/Memorize/Practice Evaluate/Appraise/Assess Compare	Construct/Assemble/Put together
	Organize/Structure/Provide definition/Plan/Chart course Strategize/Coordinate
Influence/Involve/Get participation/Publicize Promote	Create/Design/Adapt/Modify

This exercise yields a relatively comprehensive inventory of your skills. The information will better enable you to use a **skills vocabulary** when identifying your objective, writing your resume and letters, and interviewing. Your self-confidence and self-esteem should increase accordingly.

OTHER ALTERNATIVES

Several other techniques also can help you identify your motivated abilities and skills:

1. List all of your hobbies and analyze what you do in each, which ones you like the most, what skills you use, and your accomplishments.

2. Conduct a job analysis by writing about your past jobs and identifying which skills you used in each job. Cluster the skills into related categories and prioritize them according to your preferences.

3. Purchase of copy of Arthur F. Miller and Ralph T. Mattson's *The Truth About You* and work through the exercises found in the Appendix. This is an abbreviated version of the authors' SIMA (System for Identifying Motivated Abilities) technique used by their career counseling firm, People Management, Inc. (10 Station Street, Simsbury, CT 06070). If you need professional assistance, contact this firm directly. They can provide you with several alternative services consistent with the career planning philosophy and approach outlined in this chapter.

4. Complete John Holland's *"The Self-Directed Search."* You'll find it in his book, *Making Vocational Choices: A Theory of Careers* or in a separate publication entitled *The Self-Directed Search—A Guide to Educational and Vocational Planning*.

BENEFIT FROM REDUNDANCY

The self-directed MAS exercises generate similar information. They identify interests, values, abilities, and skills you already possess. While aptitude and achievement tests may yield similar information, the self-directed exercises have three major advantages over the standardized tests: less expensive, self-monitored and evaluated, and measure motivation **and** ability.

Completing each exercise demands a different investment of your time. Writing your life history and completing the Motivated Skills Exercise as well as Bolles' *"Map"* are the most time consuming. On the other hand, Holland's self-directed search can be completed in a few minutes. But the more time you invest with each technique, the more useful information you will generate. We recommend creating redundancy by using at least two or three different techniques. This will help reinforce and confirm the validity of your observations and interpretations. If you are making a mid-career change and/or have a considerable amount of experience, we recommend using the more thorough exercises. The more you put into these techniques and exercises, the greater the benefit to other stages of your job search.

STRENGTH IDENTIFICATION
INTERVIEW

Interviewee _____ **Interviewer** _____

INSTRUCTIONS: For each achievement experience, identify the **skills** and abilities which the achiever actually demonstrated. To obtain details of the experience, ask **what** was involved with the achievement and **how** the individual made the achievement happen. Avoid "why" questions which tend to mislead. Ask for examples or illustrations of what and how.

Achievement # ___   Achievement # ___   Achievement # ___

Recurring abilities and skills:

Chapter Ten

BEYOND SELF-KNOWLEDGE TO SELF-TRANSFORMATION

Not everyone desires to see their future become a replay of their past. Indeed, many people aspire to achieve goals that may initially appear to be beyond their immediate capacity. Setting ostensibly unrealistic goals, many of these people do achieve their impossible dreams.

WHY LIMIT YOURSELF?

While most people may be content in identifying their motivated abilities and skills and pursuing jobs and careers that best fit their MAS patterns, other people desire to break out of past patterns as they embark on a new and uncharted future. For this latter group, identifying one's past patterns of motivated abilities and skills may be interesting self-knowledge, but it does not help put them on the road to jobs and careers that may, for example, pay more money or offer greater and more exciting challenges than in the past.

Take, for example, the clerk typist who can type 90 words a minute and enjoys working in pleasant surroundings and with mutually supportive individuals. After 10 years of thriving in this type of job where she has really enjoyed using her best skills and abilities, she decides that making $9.00 an hour is not her idea of a swell future; she's definitely not headed for the boardroom with her typewriter in hand! As her motivation (monetary needs) and career goals change, so too does her need for a different approach to finding a job and changing careers. Self-knowledge generated by the perspective and exercises found in Chapters Seven, Eight, and Nine may be of limited usefulness as she seeks to break out of her past patterns of motivated abilities and skills.

FROM SELF-ASSESSMENT TO SELF-TRANSFORMATION

Motivation plays a central role in how and what we choose. When linked to aspirations and positive thinking, motivation can result in major changes in behavior which are largely unpredictable. This approach can and does result in major transformations for many people.

Underlining the concept of MAS is a very conservative notion that one's future behavior will largely be a reflection of one's past patterns of behavior. For some writers, this concept takes on very religious, even messianic, tones of predestination: God hath preordained your patterns when creating the "unique you"; therefore, you can't do much about these patterns other than better understand what they are and then better learn to live with them. This is an interesting and obviously controversial theory which also leads to a conservative view of where one can go from here with their life.

A form of historical determinism and probability, the MAS approach is probably valid for 85 percent of the workforce: past patterns of motivated abilities and skills are likely to recur in different work settings and situations; most people don't make significant departures from their basic patterns. In fact, most don't even try to make changes since they seem content at doing what they always do. However, this approach fails to assist individuals who are highly motivated to break out of their past patterns as they seek to embark on a new future. What, for example, can this approach do for the clerk typist who wishes to make $100,000 a year and no longer type?

Similar and rather simplistic theories of race and poverty have been used to explain why poor people are poor and are likely to stay poor in the future. Fortunately, we know better from experience.

People who are motivated to break out of their past patterns and create a new future need a different approach to jobs and careers. Indeed, self-knowledge based on traditional self-assessment exercises and tests may become an impediment to making future changes. Such information may constrain them from taking new actions that may result in major self-transformations.

Self knowledge based on traditional self-assessment exercises and tests may become an impediment to making future changes.

CHANGE

Change based on breaking out of old patterns does indeed take place, and it happens more often than we think. And change often begins when an old mind set is replaced with a new one that rejects such simplistic notions of predestination. It begins when people reject old patterns of thinking, dream the impossible, imagine future states, or set seemingly unrealistic goals for themselves and remain motivated and persist in achieving their goals. A form of breakthrough thinking, this single-minded and determined thinking is demonstrated each year by thousands of people who break out of past patterns of behavior in a process of self-transformation. They make radical departures in their jobs and careers and go on to learning and developing new patterns of motivated abilities and skills. The approaches they use are instructive for our purposes.

BREAKTHROUGH THINKING

The ability to make major changes in one's patterns of behavior, as well as achieve new goals that may depart significantly from one's past experience, is most closely associated with approaches to entrepreneurship and another school of religion. Such concepts as "the power of positive thinking," "thinking big," and "shoot for the stars" all have one central element in common—breakthrough thinking centered around setting goals and then developing strategies for achieving those goals. Positive motivations and a "can do" attitude are the most important requirements for this approach. Individuals' goals need not be "realistic" since the notion of being realistic is based upon old patterns of behavior. Such approaches do not encourage individuals to engage in self-assessment. In fact, knowing a great deal about your past may be counter-productive since one of your past patterns might be an "I can't do it" attitude of "realism." You may not be sufficiently unrealistic to be successful in whatever you do.

> *Positive motivations and a "can do" attitude are the most important requirements for this approach.*

If you want to break out of your past as you seek to acquire a new future, you must approach jobs and careers from a different approach than identified in earlier chapters. Forget doing a self-assessment that directs you toward your past patterns. Instead, focus on your interests in relation to new objectives. Just set your goals, develop the proper mind set for achieving those goals, and work like the devil to attain those goals. In so doing, you'll have to maintain a positive attitude and a high level of motivation. Above all, you must persist—despite all odds and disappointments—until you achieve your goals. You must never stop dreaming what may well become a possible dream!

THE ART OF
BEING UNREALISTIC

This self-transformation approach has numerous and well respected practitioners. Anecdotal, intuitive, and creative in nature, it stresses the importance of **changing your behavior** rather than understanding your behavior. Indeed, the problem is often one's past patterns. The way to solve this problem is to create new patterns of thinking that will lead to success. The power to do this is found within each and every person—the power to condition one's mind to think along new lines.

The techniques of self-transformation are as numerous as the practitioners of this approach. However, they all have some basic elements in common. Not only do they believe in the power of new thinking, but they chart similar strategies for achieving success:

- **Goals:** You must have a clear idea of what you want to do. Get rid of negative thoughts, discard the "I can't do it" attitude, and stop procrastinating. You can do anything you want if only you first change your attitude and set high goals to strive for. Do not be constrained by your past when setting goals. Your past is likely to be an impediment to your future if you let it interfere with your goals.

- **Planning:** You must transform your goals into a series of action plans that detail how you will go about achieving the goals on a day-to-day basis. If you set goals without a corresponding plan for implementation, you may doom your "big thinking" to frustration and failure. A plan should outline incremental changes in your behavior each day. In the long run such a plan will help create a new "unique you."

- **Discipline:** You must condition yourself to regularly take actions related to your goals and plans. Being single-minded in purpose and being persistent in what you do will be your greatest strengths in achieving your goals.

In the end, individuals are urged to make their behavior consistent with their goals. The mind should stay focused on goals since goals are the driving force for initiating change.

Essentially an individual decision-making approach, it is widely used in many circles to solve just about any problem that is defined as being within the power of individuals to tackle. This approach, for example, is used for:

- increasing personal wealth

- losing weight
- reorganizing personal finances
- motivating salespeople to increase sales
- generating more enthusiasm
- ending procrastination
- improving relationships
- getting good grades

This is a personal form of snake-oil widely publicized by charismatic speakers who attempt to rouse the masses to take charge of their lives through positive and big thinking. It's the cure-all for almost any problem that you have the power to affect, and that includes almost every problem where you are involved.

The mind should stay focused on goals since goals are the driving force for initiating change.

Once the major method used by a charismatic school of secular and religious positive thinkers who still dominate the growing "success" industry of books, videos, and audiocassettes, such as Napoleon Hill (*Think and Grow Rich*), Anthony Robbins (*Personal Power*), David Schwartz (*The Magic of Thinking Big*), Zig Ziglar (*How to Get What You Want*), Og Mandino (*Secrets of Success*), Dr. Norman Vincent Peale (*The Power of Positive Thinking*), and Dr. Robert H. Schuller (*You Can Become the Person You Want to Be*), today this approach is increasingly accepted and respected in business and government circles. Not only have many local insurance and real estate agents been raised on this approach in dealing with people, but many entrepreneurs have been motivated to leave established jobs and careers in pursuit of their business dreams. This approach has yet to make major inroads into career counseling circles where the deterministic and probabilistic MAS approach remains dominant.

What is especially interesting about this individual level problem-solving approach is its recent use as a problem-solving approach for organizations. Indeed, many businesses today use this approach to transform their operations in an increasingly competitive environment. Employees are urged to come up with new and innovative strategies and solutions to problems. Instead of analyzing the nature of problems and thus creating paralysis through analysis, they are encouraged to better define and clarify goals and then develop appropriate implementation strategies. An individual problem-solving approach has now come of age as an organizational problem-solving approach. As such, it has moved out of the hands of charismatic success advocates and into the portfolios of management consultants. As an approach to organizational change, this approach takes several forms:

- creative thinking
- brainstorming
- imaging and visualizing
- problem-solving
- breakthrough thinking
- self hypnosis

Research also shows that creative and intuitive people regularly use these methods for solving problems. The recent writings of Gerald Hadler and Shozo Hibino (*Breakthrough Thinking*) and William Fezler (*Creative Imagery*), which go beyond the anecdotal, have given this approach increased legitimacy for both individuals and organizations.

LEARNING NEW
ABILITIES AND SKILLS

The MAS approach to jobs and careers has little to say about education and training since by definition this approach is aimed at uncovering past abilities and skills and then applying them to future jobs by focusing on "transferable skills." However, the self-transformation approach recognizes the importance of acquiring new education and training as part of the process of self-transformation.

Focusing on both goals and the future, the self-transformation approach deals with the issues of education and training relating to one's interests. If, for example, your new thinking specifies being a doctor or lawyer as a career goal, then you must incorporate medical or legal education, training, and certification in your plan of action. In other words, breaking out of your past patterns may mean going back to school where you will acquire new ways of thinking and doing things relevant to your goals.

NEVER SETTLE FOR YOUR PAST

One thing the self-transformation approach stresses in contrast to the MAS approach is that you should never settle for your past. You can make significant changes if you want to. But you must have clear goals and the necessary motivation to make the changes.

But for many people, change is not what they want. They are perfectly content at having their future be a reflection of their past MAS patterns. This is what gives their lives stability, predictability, and meaning. For them, the MAS approach is most appropriate. The self-transformation approach especially appeals to those who are risk takers and entrepreneurs.

Our point here is that your future need not be a reflection of your past. If you want more out of life, then you must use an approach that will move you from where you are at present to where you want to be in the future. How your future evolves will in part be determined by the approach you use to shaping that future. At the very least, the approach must outline a plan of action.

ACQUIRING MORE
EDUCATION AND TRAINING

Do I have the necessary skills and experience required for the types of jobs that I'm interested in pursuing? How can I improve my present skill levels and acquire more experience? Do I need to learn new skills or be retrained for today's job market? Should I go back to school for a degree, diploma, or certificate? These questions are frequently asked by individuals first entering the job market or those making a job or career change. They will be central questions for individuals who use the self-transformation approach to planning their future.

It is difficult to provide simple answers to these questions. However, you first need to know what it is you want to do—specify your goals. The next chapter (Eleven) will assist you in doing this.

Second, you must conduct research to identify what skills training is really required for particular positions. Notice, we say **skills training** —not education. Although related, there is an important difference between skills training and education. Many employers are looking for specific skills rather than educational credentials. On the other hand, most educational institutions are still oriented toward transferring disciplines and subject matters to students rather than specific skills relevant to the world of work. If you fail to keep these two points in mind, you may waste a great deal of time and money on unnecessary training or seek jobs you are unqualified to perform.

You first need to know what it is you want to do.

So how should you proceed? Do the necessary self-assessment and data gathering required to answer these questions. Begin by asking yourself a key question for orienting your job search:

"What do I really want to do?"

Once you have a clear idea of your job and career goals, you will be prepared to target your job search toward particular organizations, positions, and individuals.

Assuming you know what you want to do, your next step is to gather information to determine whether you possess the necessary skills to qualify for the job. Obviously, if you are a high school graduate wishing to become a medical doctor, engineer, lawyer, or accountant, you will need several years of highly specialized training for certification in these fields. However, if you want to become an FBI agent, just what educational background, experience, and demonstrated skills do you need? Where do you find this information?

You can begin answering these questions by consulting several publications as suggested in Chapter Twelve relevant to conducting a job search. Next, talk to individuals who have a working knowledge of the particular job or career you desire. Contact people in similar positions to what you are seeking. While many educators can be helpful, they should rank as a secondary information source. Few educators are objective sources for information about education and training requirements for particular jobs. Remember, most educators are relatively isolated from day-to-day job market realities. Furthermore, educators are in the business of keeping themselves employed by recruiting more students into existing programs as well as by developing new degree and certification programs. They literally "stand where they sit" by promoting more formal education, degrees, and certification—whether or not such training and documentation is really necessary and relevant to the world of work.

Since many employers prefer conducting their own in-house training, they primarily look for individuals who are motivated, enthusiastic, trainable, and likable.

If you read materials and talk to informed individuals and employers, you will quickly learn what you need to do to be successful in your job search. If you learn you must return to school for a formal degree or certificate, your information sources will identify the most appropriate type of training you should acquire as well as recommend where best to receive the training. In many cases you will find you do not need additional training to qualify for a position. Since many employers prefer conducting their own in-house training, they primarily look for individuals who are motivated, enthusiastic, trainable, and likable.

If you must acquire new skills, keep in mind several education and training options available to you:

- Public vocational education
- Private vocational education
- Employer training

- Apprenticeship programs
- Federal employment and training programs
- Armed Forces training
- Home study schools
- Community and junior colleges
- Colleges and universities

Most of these sources emphasize practical hands-on training. Private trade schools, for example, are flourishing while university enrollments are stagnant—indicating a shift to practical skills training in education. Each alternative has various advantages and disadvantages, and costs differ considerably.

1. Public vocational education:

Public vocational education is provided through secondary, postsecondary, and adult vocational and technical programs. The emphasis in many secondary schools is to give high school students vocational training in addition to the regular academic program. Postsecondary vocational education is provided for individuals who have left high school but who are not seeking a baccalaureate degree. Adult vocational and technical programs emphasize retraining or upgrading the skills of individuals in the labor force. The traditional agricultural, trade, and industrial emphasis of vocational education has been vastly expanded to include training in distribution, health, home economics, office, and technical occupations. Most programs train individuals for specific occupations, which are outlined in the *Occupational Outlook Handbook*. Each year over 20 million people enroll in public vocational education programs.

2. Noncollegiate postsecondary vocational education:

Nearly 2 million people enroll in over 6,500 noncollegiate postsecondary schools with occupational programs each year. Most of these schools specialize in one of eight vocational areas: cosmetology/barber, business/commercial, trade, hospital, vocational/technical, allied health, arts/design, and technical. They offer programs in seven major areas: agribusiness, marketing and distribution, health, home economics, technical, business and office, and trade and industrial. Over 75 percent of these schools are privately owned institutions. And over 70 percent of the privately owned schools are either cosmetology/barber schools or business and commercial schools. Over 75 percent of the independent nonprofit schools are hospital schools. Over 1 million people complete occupational programs in noncollegiate postsecondary schools each year.

3. Employer training:

Employers spend over $40 billion a year on in-house training and education programs. This training usually involves training new employees, improving employee performance, or preparing employees for new jobs. Skilled and semi-skilled workers are trained through apprenticeship programs, learning-by-doing, and structured on-the-job instruction. Structured classroom training is increasingly offered to skilled workers by in-house trainers, professional associations, private firms, or colleges and universities. Tuition-aid programs are used frequently among firms lacking in-house training capabilities.

4. Apprenticeship programs:

Apprenticeship programs normally range from one to six years, depending on the particular trade and organization. These programs are used most extensively in the trade occupations, especially in construction and metalworking. They involve planned on-the-job training in conjunction with classroom instruction and supervision. Over 500,000 individuals are involved in apprenticeship programs each year.

5. Federal employment and training programs:

Federal employment and training programs largely function through state and local governments. The major federal program is the Job Training Partnership Act (JTPA) program. Working through Private Industry Councils (PICs), the JTPA program is designed to train the economically disadvantaged as well as displaced workers who need assistance with skills training, job search, and job relocation. JTPA also operates two youth programs—The Job Corps and the Summer Youth Employment Program. Other major Federal programs include two administered through the Employment and Training Administration: The Trade Adjustment Act program to assist workers displaced by foreign competition, and the Work Incentive (WIN) program for employable recipients of Aid to Families with Dependent Children, migrant and seasonal farm workers, Native Americans, and workers 55 and over.

6. Armed Forces Training:

The Armed Forces provide training in numerous occupational skills that may or may not be directly transferred to civilian occupations. Thousands of military recruits complete training programs in several transferable areas each year, such as computer repair, medical care, food service, metalworking, communications, and administration. Occupations unique to the military, such as infantry and guncrew, are less transferable to civilian occupations.

7. Home study (correspondence) schools:

Home study or correspondence schools provide a variety of training options. Most programs concentrate on acquiring a single skill; others may even offer a BA, MA, or Ph.D. by mail! Some programs are of questionable quality while others may be revolutionizing the education and training landscape of America. For many people, this is a convenient, inexpensive, and effective way to acquire new skills. Over 5 million people enroll in home study courses each year. Colleges and universities are quickly moving into the home study business by offering numerous televised courses for academic credit. The Public Broadcast System (PBS) offers several home study courses through its Adult Learning Service: computer literacy and applications, basic skills and personal enrich-

ment, sales and customer service, effective communication
skills, and management skills.

8. Community and junior colleges:

Community and junior colleges in recent years have broad-
ened their missions from primarily preparing individuals for
university degree programs to preparing them with skills for
the job market. Accordingly, more of their programs emphasize vocational and occupational curriculums, such as data
processing or dental hygiene, which are typically two-year
programs resulting in an associate degree. Community and
junior colleges will probably continue to expand their program offerings as they further adjust to the employment
needs of communities. Nearly 5 million students enroll in
community and junior college programs each year.

9. Colleges and universities:

Colleges and universities continue to provide the traditional
four-year and graduate degree programs in various subject
fields. While many of the fields are occupational-specific,
such as engineering, law, medicine, and business, many
other fields are not. The exact relationship of the degree
program to the job market varies with different disciplines.
As noted earlier, in recent years, graduates of many programs have had difficulty finding employment in their chosen
fields. This is particularly true for students who only have a
generalist background in the liberal arts. During the past
decade many colleges and universities have adjusted to
declining enrollments by offering several nontraditional oc-
cupational-related courses and programs. Continuing education, special skills training courses, short courses, evening
course offerings, "telecourses," and workshops and seminars
on job-related matters have become popular with nontraditional, older students who seek specific skills training rather
than degrees. At the same time, traditional academic programs are placing greater emphasis on internships and cooperative education programs in order to give students work
experience related to their academic programs.

Additional training programs may be sponsored by local governments, professional associations, women's centers, YWCA's, and religious and civic groups. As training and retraining become more acceptable to the general public, we can expect different forms and types of training programs to be sponsored by various groups.

We also can expect a revolution in the training field, closely related to high-tech developments. Televised education and training courses should continue to increase in number and scope. Computer-based training, similar in some respects to traditional home study programs, will become more prevalent as computer software and interactive video training packages are developed in response to the new technology and the rising demand for skills training.

Individuals in tomorrow's education training markets will become examples of Toffler's "prosumer society": in a decentralized information market, individuals will choose what training they most desire as well as control when and where they will receive it. With the development of interactive video and computer training programs, individuals will manage the training process in a more efficient and effective manner than with the more centralized, time consuming, and expensive use of traditional student-teacher classroom instruction. This type of training may eventually make many of the previously discussed categories of education and training obsolete.

BECOME AN INFORMED CONSUMER

Several resources can help you decide which training path is more appropriate for you. If you use the *Discover II* computerized career planning system, you will find it includes a section that matches education and training programs with career interests. A few other computer software programs also match career interests with education and training programs. Contact your local secondary school, community college, or library for information on these programs.

You should begin your search for useful education and training information by consulting several useful publications. The major sources will be found in the reference section of libraries as well as in guidance offices and career planning centers of schools, colleges, universities, and specialized employment assistance centers. Most of these organizations maintain catalogues, directories, and files listing educational and training opportunities.

Two useful sources for information on education and training programs are *Peterson's Guides* and *Barron's Educational Series* which publish several excellent directories. Most of the directories are updated annually and include basic information on choosing programs and institutions best suited to your interests. Among the many titles offered by Peterson's and Barron's are:

- *Guide to Four-Year Colleges*
- *Guide to Two-Year Colleges*
- *The College Money Handbook*
- *Guides to Graduate Study:*
  —*Graduate and Professional Programs*
  —*Humanities and Social Sciences*
  —*Biological Agricultural and Health Sciences*
  —*Physical Sciences and Mathematics*
  —*Engineering and Applied Sciences*
- *Regional Guides to Colleges*
  —*Middle Atlantic*
  —*Midwest*
  —*New England*
  —*New York*
  —*Southeast*
  —*Southwest*
  —*West*
- *Winning Money for College*
- *How to Write Your Way into College*
- *Job Opportunities for Engineering, Science, and Computer Graduates*
- *Job Opportunities for Business and Liberal Arts Graduates*
- *Guide to Medical and Dental Schools*
- *How to Prepare for the SAT*
- *Guide to Law Schools*
- *Profiles of American Colleges*
- *Guide to Graduate Business Schools*
- *Applying to Colleges and Universities in the United States*
- *Applying to Graduate School in the United States*
- *Competitive Colleges*
- *Colleges With Programs for Learning-Disabled Students*
- *National College Databank*
- *Handbook for College Admissions*

- *Guide to College Admissions*
- *How the Military Will Help You Pay for College*
- *Corporate Tuition Aid Programs*
- *Graduate Education Directory*

Most major libraries have copies of these publications in their reference section. If you cannot find them in your local library, check with your local bookstore or contact the publishers directly: Peterson's Guides, P.O. Box 2123, Princeton, NJ 08543-2123, Tel. 609/924/5338; and Barron's Educational Series, 250 Wireless Blvd., Hauppauge, NY 11788, Tel. 516/434-3311.

If you decide you need to acquire a specific skill, consult various professional or trade associations; many can provide you with a list of reputable institutions providing skills training in particular fields. The names, addresses, and telephone numbers of all major associations are listed in the *Encyclopedia of Associations* (Gale Publishers) and *National Trade and Professional Associations* (Columbia Books), two extremely useful directories found in the reference section of most libraries.

The U.S. Department of Labor's *Occupational Outlook Handbook* also lists useful names and addresses relating to employment training in specific fields. Consult the *"Where to Go For More Information"* section in the latest edition of this biannual directory. This book is also available in most libraries and can be purchased from Impact Publications by completing the order form at the end of this book.

For information on **private trade and technical schools**, be sure to contact the National Association of Trade and Technical Schools (NATTS). They produce three publications you may find useful: *Handbook of Accredited Private Trade and Technical Schools* and a series of pamphlets, including *How to Choose a Career and a Career School*. Write or call NATTS for information on these publications: NATTS, 2251 Wisconsin Ave., NW, Washington, DC 20007, Tel. 202/333-1021.

For information on **apprenticeship programs**, contact the Bureau of Apprenticeships and Training (BAT), U.S. Department of Labor, 200 Constitution Ave., NW, Washington, DC 20210, Tel. 202/535-0545. BAT offices are also found in each state. To find if there is a BAT office near you, consult the White Pages of your telephone directory under "United States Government—Department of Labor." Your local library and public employment service office should also have information on apprenticeship programs. For women interested in apprenticeship opportunities, send a self-addressed mailing label to the Women's Bureau, U.S. Department of Labor (200 Constitution Ave., NW, Washington, DC 20210, Tel. 202/523-6631) to receive a free copy of their publication, *A Woman's Guide to Apprenticeship*.

If you are interested in **home study and correspondence courses,** contact the National Home Study Council (NHSC) for information on home study programs. NHSC distributes copies of a useful publication entitled *Directory of Accredited Home Study Programs*. For information on this and other NHSC publications, contact: National Home Study Council, 1601 18th St., NW, Washington, DC 20009, Tel. 202/234-5100.

You also need to determine the quality and suitability of these education and training programs. Many programs have reputations for fraud, abuse, and incompetence—primarily take your time and money in exchange for broken promises. After all, this is a business transaction—your money in exchange for their services. As an informed consumer, you must demand quality performance for your money. Therefore, when contacting a particular institution, ask to speak to former students and graduates. Write to the Council on Postsecondary Accreditation (One Dupont Circle, Suite 760, Washington, DC 20036) to inquire about the school's credentials. Focus your attention on the **results** or **outcomes** the institution achieves. Instead of asking how many faculty have Master or Ph.D. degrees, or how many students are enrolled, ask these performance questions:

- What are last year's graduates doing today?
- Where do they work and for whom?
- How much do they earn?
- How many were placed in jobs through this institution?

Institutions that can answer these questions focus on **performance**. Beware of those that can't answer these questions, for they may not be doing an adequate job to meet your needs.

Most colleges and universities will provide assistance to adult learners. Contact student services, continuing education, academic advising, adult services, or women's offices at your local community college, college, or university. Be sure to talk to present and former students about the **expectations and results** of the programs for them.

Always remember that educators are first in the business of keeping themselves employed and, second, in the business of delivering educational services. And today, more than ever, educational institutions need students to keep their programs alive. Don't necessarily expect professional educators to be objective about your future vis-a-vis their interests, skills, and programs. At the very least, you must do a critical evaluation of their programs and services.

If you need further assistance, contact a local branch of the National Center for Educational Brokering. While there is no national clearinghouse to help you match your goals with appropriate educational programs, NCEB can assist you nonetheless. NCEB counselors will help you identify your goals and career alternatives. For information on the center nearest you, contact the National Center for Educational Brokering, 329 9th St., San Francisco, CA 94103, Tel. 415/626-2378.

Other useful sources of information on education and training programs are your telephone book and employers. Look under "Schools" in the Yellow Pages of your telephone directory. Call the schools and ask them to send you literature and application forms and discuss the relevance of their programs to the job market. You should also talk to employers and individuals who have work experience in the field that interests you. Ask them how best to acquire the necessary skills for particular occupations. Most important, thoroughly research education and training alternatives before you invest any money, time, or effort.

Thoroughly research education and training alternatives before you invest any money, time, or effort.

Beware of education and training myths. Additional education and training is not always the answer for entry or advancement within the job market. First, you should identify what it is you want to do and then identify what it is you need to do to get what you want. Indeed, employers spend over $40 billion each year on employee training and retraining—much of which is spent because of the failure of traditional educational institutions. You may find it is best to get into a particular organization that provides excellent training for its employees. Most of the best run corporations rely on their own in-house training rather than on institutions outside the corporation. Even government is providing more and more training for its employees, although it still places a great deal of emphasis on formal educational credentials for entry into the government service.

Chapter Eleven

SET GOALS AND
STATE YOUR OBJECTIVE

Goals and objectives are statements of what you want to do in the future. When combined with an assessment of your interests, values, abilities and skills and targeted on specific jobs, they give your job search needed direction and meaning for the purpose of targeting specific employers. Without them, your job search may founder as you present a image of uncertainty and confusion to potential employers.

When you identify your strengths, you also create the necessary data base and vocabulary for developing your job objective. Using this vocabulary, you should be able to communicate to employers that you are a talented and purposeful individual who achieves **results**.

If you fail to do the preliminary self-assessment work necessary for developing a clear objective, you will probably wander aimlessly in the job market looking for interesting jobs you might fit into. Your goal, instead, should be to find a job or career that is compatible with your interests, motivations, skills, and talents as well as related to a vision of your future. In other words, try to find a job fit for you and your future rather than try to fit into a job that happens to be advertised and for which you think you can qualify.

EXAMINE YOUR PAST,
PRESENT, AND FUTURE

Depending on how you approach your job search, your goals can be largely a restatement of your past MAS patterns or a vision of your future. If you base your job search on an analysis of your motivated abilities and skills, you may prefer restating your past patterns as your present and future goals. On the other hand, you may want to establish a vision of your future and set goals that motivate you to achieve that vision through a process of self-transformation.

The type of goals you choose to establish will involve different processes. However, the strongest goals will be those that combine your motivated abilities and skills with a realistic vision of your future.

ORIENT YOURSELF TOWARD
THE NEEDS OF EMPLOYERS

Your objective should be a concise statement of what you want to do and what you have to offer to an employer. The position you seek is "what you want to do"; your qualifications are "what you have to offer." Your objective should state your strongest qualifications for meeting employer's needs. It should communicate what you have to offer an employer without emphasizing what you expect the employer to do for you. In other words, your objective should be **work-centered**, not self-centered; it should not contain trite terms which emphasize what you want, such as give me a(n) "opportunity for advancement," "position working with people," "progressive company," or "creative position." Such terms are viewed as "canned" job search language which say little of value about you. Above all, your objective should reflect your honesty and integrity; it should not be "hyped."

Identifying what it is you want to do can be one of the most difficult job search tasks. Indeed, most job hunters lack clear objectives. Many engage in a random, and somewhat mindless, search for jobs by identifying available job opportunities and then adjusting their skills and objectives to "fit" specific job openings. While you will get a job using this approach, you may be misplaced and unhappy with what you find. You will fit into a job rather than find a job that is fit for you.

Knowing what you want to do can have numerous benefits. First, you define the job market rather than let it define you. The inherent fragmentation and chaos of the job market should be advantageous for you, because it enables you to systematically organize job opportunities around your specific objectives and skills. Second, you will communicate professionalism to prospective employers. They will receive a precise indication of your interests, qualifications, and purposes, which places you ahead of most other applicants. Third, being purposeful means being able to communicate to employers what you want to do. Employers are not interested in hiring indecisive and confused individuals. They want to know what it is you can do for them. With a clear objective, based upon a thorough understanding of your motivated skills and interests, you can take control of the situation as you demonstrate your value to employers.

Finally, few employers really know what they want in a candidate. Like most job seekers, employers lack clear employment objectives and knowledge about how the job market operates. Thus, if you know what you want and can help the employer define his or her "needs" as your objective, you will have achieved a tremendously advantageous position in the job market.

BE PURPOSEFUL
AND REALISTIC

Your objective should communicate that you are a **purposeful individual who achieves results**. It can be stated over different time periods as well as at various levels of abstraction and specificity. You can identify short, intermediate, and long-range objectives and very general to very specific objectives. Whatever the case, it is best to know your prospective audience before deciding on the type of objective. Your objective should reflect your career interests as well as employers' needs.

Objectives also should be **realistic**. You may want to become President of the United States or solve all the world's problems. However, these objectives are probably unrealistic. While they may represent your ideals and fantasies, you need to be more realistic in terms of what you can personally accomplish in the immediate future. What, for example, are you prepared to deliver to prospective employers over the next few months? While it is good to set challenging objectives, you can overdo it. Refine your objective by thinking about the next major step or two you would like to make in your career advancement—not some grandiose leap outside reality!

> *Your objective should communicate that you are a purposeful individual who achieves results. It gives meaning and direction to all other activities.*

PROJECT YOURSELF
INTO THE FUTURE

Even after identifying your abilities and skills, specifying an objective can be the most difficult and tedious step in the job search process; it can stall the resume writing process indefinitely. This simple one-sentence, 25-word statement can take days or weeks to formulate and clearly define. Yet, it must be specified prior to writing the resume and engaging in other job search steps. An objective gives meaning and direction to all other activities.

Your objective should be viewed as a function of several influences. Since you want to build upon your strengths and you want to be realistic, your abilities and skills will play a central role in formulating your work objective. At the same time, you do not want your objective to become a function solely of your past accomplishments and skills. You may be very skilled in certain areas, but you may not want to use these skills in the future. As a result, your values and interests filter which skills you will or will not incorporate into your work objective.

Overcoming the problem of historical determinism—your future merely reflecting your past—requires incorporating additional components into defining your objective. One of the most important is your ideals, fantasies, or dreams. Everyone engages in these, and sometimes they come true. Your ideals, fantasies, or dreams may include making $1,000,000 by age 45; owning a Mercedes-Benz and a Porsche; taking trips to Rio, Hong Kong, and Rome; owning your own business; developing financial independence; writing a best-selling novel; solving major social problems; or winning the Nobel Peace Prize. If your fantasies require more money than you are now making, you will need to incorporate monetary considerations into your work objective.

You can develop realistic objectives many different ways. We don't claim to have a new or magical formula, only one which has worked for many individuals. We assume you are capable of making intelligent career decisions if given sufficient data. Using redundancy once again, our approach is designed to provide you with sufficient corroborating data from several sources and perspectives so that you can make preliminary decisions. If you follow our steps in setting a realistic objective, you should be able to give your job search clear direction.

Four major steps are involved in developing a work objective. Each step can be implemented in a variety of ways:

STEP 1: Develop or obtain basic data on your functional/transferable skills, which we discussed in Chapter Seven.

STEP 2: Acquire corroborating data about yourself from others, tests, and an analysis of yourself. Several resources are available for this purpose:

A. From others: Ask three to five individuals whom you know well to evaluate you according to the questions in the "Strength Evaluation" form on page 134. Explain to these people that you believe their candid appraisal will help you gain a better understanding of your strengths and weaknesses from the perspectives of others. Make copies of this form and ask your evaluators to complete and return it to a designated third party who will share the information—but not the respondent's name—with you.

STRENGTH EVALUATION

TO: _____

FROM: _____

    I am going through a career assessment process and thought you would be an appropriate person to ask for assistance. Would you please candidly respond to the questions below? Your comments will be given to me by the individual designed below; s/he will not reveal your name. Your comments will be used for advising purposes only. Thank you.

What are my strengths?

What weak areas might I need to improve?

In your opinion, what do I need in a job or career to make me satisfied?

Please return to: _____

B. From vocational tests: Although we prefer self-generated data, vocationally-oriented tests can help clarify, confirm, and translate your understanding of yourself into occupational directions. If you decide to use vocational tests, contact a professional career counselor who can administer and interpret the tests. We recommend several of the following tests:

- Strong-Campbell Interest Inventory
- Myers-Briggs Type Indicator
- Edwards Personal Preference Schedule
- Kuder Occupational Interest Survey
- APTICOM
- Jackson Vocational Interest Survey
- Ramak Inventory
- Vocational Interest Inventory
- Career Assessment Inventory
- Temperament and Values Inventory

C. From yourself: Numerous alternatives are available for you to practice redundancy. Refer to the exercises in Chapter Eight that assist you in identifying your work values, job frustrations and dissatisfactions, things you love to do, things you enjoy most about work, and your preferred interpersonal environments.

STEP 3: Project your values and preferences into the future by completing simulation and creative thinking exercises:

A. Ten Million Dollar Exercise: First, assume that you are given a $10,000,000 gift; now you don't have to work. Since the gift is restricted to your use only, you cannot give any part of it away. What will you do with your time! At first? Later on? Second, assume that you are given another $10,000,000, but this time you are required to give it all away. What kinds of causes,

organizations, charities, etc. would you support?
Complete the following form in which you answer
these questions:

WHAT WILL I DO WITH
TWO $10,000,000 GIFTS?

First gift is restricted to my use only:

_____

_____

_____

_____

_____

_____

_____

Second gift must be given away:

_____

_____

_____

_____

_____

_____

SOURCE: John C. Crystal, *"Life/Work Planning Workshop"*

B. Obituary Exercise: Make a list of the most important things you would like to do or accomplish before you die. Two alternatives are available for doing this. First, make a list in response to this lead-in statement: *"Before I die, I want to..."*

BEFORE I DIE, I WANT TO . . .

1. _____

   _____

2. _____

   _____

3. _____

   _____

4. _____

   _____

5. _____

   _____

6. _____

   _____

7. _____

   _____

8. _____

   _____

9. _____

   _____

10. _____

   _____

Second, write a newspaper article which is actually your obituary for ten years from now. Stress your accomplishments over the coming ten year period.

MY OBITUARY

Obituary for Mr./Ms. _____ to appear in the _____ Newspaper in 2000.

_____

_____

_____

_____

_____

_____

_____

_____

_____

_____

_____

_____

C. My Ideal Work Week: Starting with Monday, place each day of the week on the headings of seven sheets of paper. Develop a daily calendar with 30-minute intervals, beginning at 7am and ending at mid-night. Your calendar should consist of a 118-hour week. Next, beginning at 7am on Monday (sheet one), identify the **ideal activities** you would enjoy doing, or need to do for each 30-minute segment during the day. Assume you are capable of doing anything; you have no constraints except those you impose on yourself. Furthermore, assume that your work schedule consists of 40 hours per week. How will you fill your time? Be specific.

MY IDEAL WORK WEEK

Monday
am

7:00 _____

7:30 _____

8:00 _____

8:30 _____

9:00 _____

9:30 _____

10:00 _____

10:30 _____

11:00 _____

11:30 _____

12:00 _____

p.m. _____

12:30 _____

1:00 _____

1:30 _____

2:00 _____

pm

4:00 _____

4:30 _____

5:00 _____

5:30 _____

6:00 _____

6:30 _____

7:00 _____

7:30 _____

8:00 _____

8:30 _____

9:00 _____

9:30 _____

10:00 _____

10:30 _____

11:00 _____

11:30 _____

2:30 _____   12:00 _____

3:00 _____   Continue for Tuesday,
                            Wednesday, Thursday,
3:30 _____   and Friday

D. My Ideal Job Description: Develop your
ideal future job. Be sure you include:

- Specific interests you want to
  build into your job
- Work responsibilities
- Working conditions
- Earnings and benefits
- Interpersonal environment
- Working circumstances, opportunities,
  and goals

Use *"My Ideal Job Specifications"* on page 141
to outline your ideal job. After completing this
exercise, synthesize the job and write a detailed
paragraph which describes the kind of job you
would most enjoy:

DESCRIPTION OF MY IDEAL JOB

_____

_____

_____

_____

_____

_____

_____

_____

MY IDEAL JOB SPECIFICATIONS

Job Interests	Work Responsibilities	Working Conditions	Earnings/ Benefits	Interpersonal Environment	Circumstances/ Opportunities/ Goals

STEP 4: **Test your objective against reality. Evaluate and refine it by conducting market research, a force field analysis, library research, and informational interviews.**

A. Market Research: Four steps are involved in conducting this research:

1. Products or services: Based upon all other assessment activities, make a list of what you **do** or **make**:

PRODUCTS/SERVICES
I DO OR MAKE

1. _____
2. _____
3. _____
4. _____
5. _____
6. _____
7. _____
8. _____
9. _____
10. _____

2. Market: Identify who needs, wants, or buys what you do or make. Be specific. Include individuals, groups, and organizations. Then, identify **what** specific **needs** your products or services fill. Next, assess the **results** you achieve with your products or services.

THE MARKET FOR MY PRODUCTS/SERVICES

Individuals, groups, organizations needing me:

1. _____
2. _____
3. _____
4. _____
5. _____

Needs I fulfill:

1. _____
2. _____
3. _____
4. _____
5. _____

Results/Outcomes/Impacts of my products/services:

1. _____
2. _____
3. _____
4. _____
5. _____

3. New Markets: Brainstorm a list of **who else** needs your products or services. Think about ways of expanding your market. Next, list any new needs your current or new market has which you might be able to fill:

DEVELOPING NEW NEEDS

Who else needs my products/services?

1. _____
2. _____
3. _____
4. _____
5. _____

New ways to expand my market:

1. _____
2. _____
3. _____
4. _____
5. _____

New needs I should fulfill:

1. _____
2. _____
3. _____
4. _____
5. _____

4. New products and/or services: List any new products or services you can offer and any new needs you can satisfy:

NEW PRODUCTS/SERVICES I CAN OFFER

1. _____

2. _____

3. _____

4. _____

5. _____

NEW NEEDS I CAN MEET

1. _____

2. _____

3. _____

4. _____

5. _____

B. Force Field Analysis: Once you have developed a tentative or firm objective, force field analysis can help you understand the various internal and external forces affecting the achievement of your objective. Force field analysis follows a specific sequence of activities:

- Clearly state your objective or course of action.

- List the positive and negative forces affecting your objective. Specify the internal and external forces working **for** and **against** you in terms of who, what, where, when, and how much. Estimate the impact of each force upon your objective.

- Analyze the forces. Assess the importance of each force upon your objective and its probable affect upon you. Some forces may be irrelevant to your goal. You may need additional information to make a thorough analysis.

- Maximize positive forces and minimize negative ones. Identify actions you can take to strengthen positive forces and to neutralize, overcome, or reverse negative forces. Focus on the key forces which are real, important, and probable.

- Assess the feasibility of attaining your objective and, if necessary, modifying it in light of new information.

C. Conduct Library Research: This research should strengthen and clarify your objective. Consult various reference materials on alternative jobs and careers:

Career & Job Alternatives:
- *Dictionary of Occupational Titles*
- *Encyclopedia of Careers a Vocational Guidance,*
- *Guide for Occupational Exploration*
- *Occupational Outlook Handbook*
- *Occupational Outlook Quarterly*

Industrial Directories:
- *Bernard Klein's Guide to American Directories*
- *Dun and Bradstreet's Middle Market Directory*
- *Dun and Bradstreet's Million Dollar Directory*

- *Encyclopedia of Business Information Sources*
- *Geography Index*
- *Poor's Register of Corporations, Directors, and Executives*
- *Standard Directory of Advertisers*
- *The Standard Periodical Directory*
- *Standard and Poor's Industrial Index*
- *Standard Rate and Data Business Publications Directory*
- *Thomas' Register of American Manufacturers*

Associations:
- *Directory of Professional and Trade Associations*
- *Encyclopedia of Associations*

Government Sources:
- *The Book of the States*
- *Congressional Directory*
- *Congressional Staff Directory*
- *Congressional Yellow Book*
- *Federal Directory*
- *Federal Yellow Book*
- *Municipal Yearbook*
- *Taylor's Encyclopedia of Government Officials*
- *United National Yearbook*
- *United States Government Manual*
- *Washington Information Directory*

Newspapers:
- *The Wall Street Journal*
- Major city newspapers
- Trade newspapers
- Any city newspaper— especially the Sunday edition.

Business Publications:
- *Barron's, Business Week, Business World, Forbes, Fortune, Harvard Business Review, Money, Time, Newsweek, U.S. News and World Report*

Other Resources:	▪ Trade journals (refer to the *Directory of Special Libraries and Information Centers* and *Subject Collections: A Guide to Specialized Libraries of Businesses, Governments, and Associations*).
	▪ Publications of Chambers of Commerce; State Manufacturing Associations; and federal, state, and local government agencies
	▪ Telephone books—The Yellow Pages
	▪ Trade books on *"How to get a job"*

4. Conduct Informational Interviews: This may be the most useful way to clarify and refine your objective. We'll discuss this procedure in the next chapter.

After completing these steps, you will have identified what it is you **can** do (abilities and skills), enlarged your thinking to include what it is you would **like** to do (aspirations), and probed the realities of implementing your objective. Thus, setting a realistic work objective is a function of the diverse considerations represented on page 149.

Your work objective is a function of both subjective and objective information as well as idealism and realism. We believe the strongest emphasis should be placed on your competencies and should include a broad data-base. Your work objective is realistic in that it is tempered by your past experiences, accomplishments, skills, and current research. An objective formulated in this manner permits you to think beyond your past experiences.

STATE A FUNCTIONAL OBJECTIVE

Your job objective should be oriented toward skills and results or outcomes. You can begin by stating a functional job objective at two different levels: a general objective and a specific one for communicating your qualifications to employers both on resumes and in interviews. Thus, this objective setting process sets the stage for other

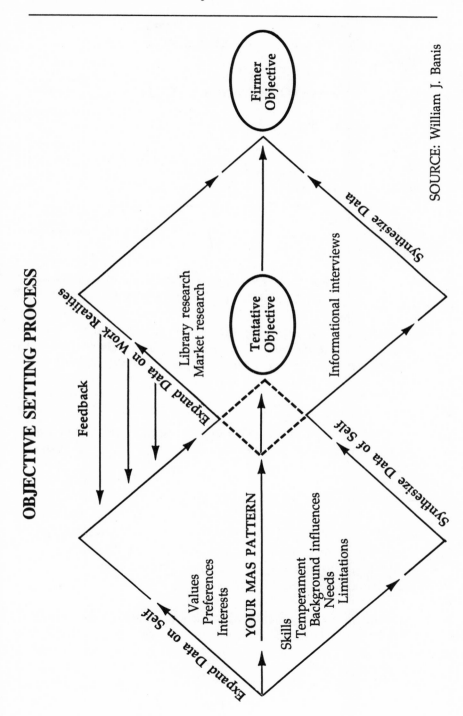

OBJECTIVE SETTING PROCESS

SOURCE: William J. Banis

Firmer Objective

Tentative Objective

Synthesize Data

Library research
Market research

Informational interviews

Expand Data on Work Realities

Feedback

Synthesize Data of Self

Values
Preferences
Interests

YOUR MAS PATTERN

Skills
Temperament
Background influences
Needs
Limitations

Expand Data on Self

key job search activities. For the general objective, begin with the
statement:

———— STATING YOUR GENERAL OBJECTIVE ————

*I would like a job where I can use my ability to _____
which will result in _____ .*

SOURCE: Richard Germann and Peter Arnold, **Bernard Haldane Associates
Job & Career Building** (New York: Harper and Row, 1980), 54-55.

The objective in this statement is both a **skill** and an **outcome**. For
example, you might state:

**———— SKILLS-BASED AND ————
RESULTS-ORIENTED OBJECTIVE**

*I would like a job where my experience in program develop-
ment, supported by innovative decision-making and systems
engineering abilities, will result in an expanded clientele and a
more profitable organization.*

At a second level you may wish to re-write this objective in order
to target it at various consulting firms. For example, on your resume
it becomes:

———— JOB TARGETED OBJECTIVE ————

*An increasingly responsible research position in consulting,
where proven decision-making and system engineering abilities
will be used for improving organizational productivity.*

The following are examples of weak and strong objective statements. Various styles are also presented:

WEAK OBJECTIVES

Management position which will use business administration degree and will provide opportunities for rapid advancement.

A position in social services which will allow me to work with people in a helping capacity.

A position in Personnel Administration with a progressive firm.

Sales Representative with opportunity for advancement.

STRONG OBJECTIVES

*To use computer science training in **software development** for designing and implementing operating systems.*

A public relations position which will maximize opportunities to develop and implement programs, to organize people and events, and to communicate positive ideas and images. Effective in public speaking and in managing a publicity/promotional campaign.

A position as a General Sales Representative with a pharmaceutical house which will use chemistry background and ability to work on a self-directed basis in managing a marketing territory.

A position in data analysis where skills in mathematics, computer programming, and deductive reasoning will contribute to new systems development.

Retail Management position which will use sales/customer service experience and creative abilities for product display and merchandising. Long term goal: Progression to merchandise manager with corporate-wide responsibilities for product line.

Responsible position in investment research and analysis. Interests and skills include securities analysis, financial planning, and portfolio management. Long range goal: to become a Chartered Financial Analyst.

It is important to relate your objective to your audience. While you definitely want a good job, your audience wants to know what you can do for them. Remember, your objective should be work-centered, not self-centered.

Chapter Twelve

ALTERNATIVE JOBS AND CAREERS

Once you have a clear idea of what you do well and enjoy doing as well as what you would like to do in the future, you need to link this information on yourself to the world of work. For in the end, you need to know what jobs are most appropriate for someone with your "qualifications." You do this through a combination of investigative techniques that put you close to real world of work and employers.

LINKAGE SYSTEMS

There are no magical formulas for relating information on yourself to specific jobs. While some employment specialists have attempted to develop elaborate systems that relate individual personality, interests, values, abilities, skills, and objectives to different job titles, most such efforts are highly generalized. At best they give you a general overview of the types of jobs you might be most interested in pursuing. Few provide you with the detailed information necessary for making informed career decisions.

Nonetheless, you should examine some of these systems for the purpose of narrowing your job choices to a manageable whole for further investigation. They come in many forms, from simple checklists for matching individual characteristics to job titles to more intensive forms of content analysis requiring a high level of analytical skills along with information on specific jobs. The U.S. Department of Labor, for example, has devised a job-matching chart that relates information on the individual to nearly 200 of the most popular and rapidly growing jobs in the United States. The jobs are clustered into related occupational areas as illustrated on pages 155-161. Further information on these and other related jobs is found in two of the Department of Labor's most widely used occupational reference works: *Occupational Outlook Handbook* and *Dictionary of Occupational Titles*. Both books are available through Impact Publications.

The *Guide For Occupational Exploration* also attempts to relate information on individuals to specific occupational fields. Focusing primarily on individual interests, but also including skills and abilities, the *Guide* identifies numerous jobs outlined to the *Dictionary of Occupational Titles* and relates these to information on individuals. This ambitious attempt to relate the descriptive nature of the *Dictionary* relevant to individual interests and skills provides a wealth of information on jobs. For individual occupations, it includes numerous checklists that help individuals focus on the interests, skills, abilities, and educational training required for each job.

Less ambitious and more eclectic systems are occasionally developed by enterprising writers and employment specialists. One of the most popular ones is outlined in Barry and Linda Gale's book, *Discover What You're Best At*. Dubbed the *"National Career Aptitude System,"* the author's so-called "system" is a series of self-administered multiple choice tests that examine business, clerical, logical, mechanical, numerical, and social aptitudes. These, in turn, are clustered and then related to some very general occupational titles. The book also includes brief descriptions of more than 1,100 careers which are also found in the *Dictionary of Occupational Titles* and the *Occupational Outlook Handbook*. The latest edition of this book assigns occupational cluster codes to each occupational description.

Practitioners of the motivated abilities and skills approach to career discovery also stress the importance of related self-assessment information to specific jobs. One of the most explicit and labor intensive approaches is outlined in Miller and Mattson's *The Truth About You*. Their analytical method, trademarked as the SIMA technique for assessing motivated abilities, is also used for "matching" one's motivated abilities with specific jobs. This requires identi-

DEPARTMENT OF LABOR JOB MATCHING SYSTEM*

	Job requirements								Work environment					Occupational characteristics			
	1. Leadership/persuasion	2. Helping/instructing others	3. Problem-solving/creativity	4. Initiative	5. Work as part of a team	6. Frequent public contact	7. Manual dexterity	8. Physical stamina	9. Hazardous	10. Outdoors	11. Confined	12. Geographically concentrated	13. Part-time	14. Earnings	15. Employment growth	16. Number of new jobs through 1995 (in thousands)	17. Entry requirements
Executive, Administrative, and Managerial Occupations																	
Managers and Administrators																	
Bank officers and managers	●	●	●	●	●	●						●		H	H	119	H
Health services managers	●	●	●	●	●	●								H	H	147	H
Hotel managers and assistants	●	●	●	●	●	●								[1]	H	21	M
School principals and assistant principals	●	●	●	●	●	●								H	L	12	H
Management Support Occupations																	
Accountants and auditors		●	●		●	●						●		H	H	307	H
Construction and building inspectors		●	●	●	●		●		●					M	L	4	M
Inspectors and compliance officers, except construction		●	●	●	●		●		●					H	L	10	M
Personnel, training, and labor relations specialists	●	●	●	●	●	●								H	M	34	H
Purchasing agents	●		●		●	●								H	M	36	H
Underwriters			●											H	H	17	H
Wholesale and retail buyers	●	●	●	●	●									M	M	28	H
Engineers, Surveyors, and Architects																	
Architects			●	●	●	●	●							H	H	25	H
Surveyors	●				●		●	●		●				M	M	6	M
Engineers																	
Aerospace engineers			●	●	●							●		H	H	14	H
Chemical engineers			●	●	●									H	H	13	H
Civil engineers			●	●	●									H	H	46	H
Electrical and electronics engineers			●	●	●									H	H	206	H
Industrial engineers			●	●	●									H	H	37	H
Mechanical engineers			●	●	●									H	H	81	H
Metallurgical, ceramics, and materials engineers			●	●	●									H	H	4	H
Mining engineers			●	●	●									H	L	[2]	H
Nuclear engineers			●	●	●									H	L	1	H
Petroleum engineers			●	●	●							●		H	M	4	H
Natural Scientists and Mathematicians																	
Computer and Mathematical Occupations																	
Actuaries			●	●							●	●		H	H	4	H
Computer systems analysts	●	●	●	●	●							●		H	H	212	H
Mathematicians			●	●										H	M	4	H
Statisticians			●	●										H	M	4	H

[1] Estimates not available.
[2] Less than 500.

*Reprinted from the *Occupational Outlook Quarterly*, Fall 1986. U.S. Department of Labor Bureau of Labor Statistics.

	Job requirements								Work environment					Occupational characteristics			
	1. Leadership/persuasion	2. Helping/instructing others	3. Problem-solving/creativity	4. Initiative	5. Work as part of a team	6. Frequent public contact	7. Manual dexterity	8. Physical stamina	9. Hazardous	10. Outdoors	11. Confined	12. Geographically concentrated	13. Part-time	14. Earnings	15. Employment growth	16. Number of new jobs through 1995 (in thousands)	17. Entry requirements
Physical Scientists			•	•										H	M		H
Chemists			•	•										H	L	9	H
Geologists and geophysicists			•	•	•					•		•		H	M	7	H
Meteorologists			•	•	•									H	M	1	H
Physicists and astronomers			•	•										H	L	2	H
Life Scientists																	
Agricultural scientists			•	•										'	M	3	H
Biological scientists			•	•										H	M	10	H
Foresters and conservation scientists	•	•	•	•				•	•	•				H	L	2	H
Social Scientists, Social Workers, Religious Workers, and Lawyers																	
Lawyers	•	•	•	•	•	•								H	H	174	H
Social Scientists and Urban Planners																	
Economists			•	•										H	M	7	H
Psychologists		•	•	•		•								H	H	21	H
Sociologists			•	•		•								H	L	²	H
Urban and regional planners	•		•	•		•								H	L	2	H
Social and Recreation Workers																	
Social workers	•	•	•	•	•	•								M	H	75	H
Recreation workers	•	•	•	•	•	•	•	•		•			•	L	H	26	M
Religious Workers																	
Protestant ministers	•	•	•	•	•	•								L	'	'	H
Rabbis	•	•	•	•	•	•								H	'	'	H
Roman Catholic priests	•	•	•	•	•	•								L	'	'	H
Teachers, Counselors, Librarians, and Archivists																	
Kindergarten and elementary school teachers	•	•	•	•	•	•	•	•						M	H	281	H
Secondary school teachers	•	•	•	•	•	•		•						M	L	48	H
Adult and vocational education teachers	•	•	•	•	•	•	•	•					•	M	M	48	H
College and university faculty	•	•	•	•	•	•		•					•	H	L	−77	H
Counselors	•	•	•	•	•	•								M	M	29	H
Librarians	•	•	•	•	•	•		•					•	M	L	16	H
Archivists and curators			•	•	•									M	L	1	H
Health Diagnosing and Treating Practitioners																	
Chiropractors	•	•	•	•	•	•	•							H	H	9	H
Dentists	•	•	•	•	•	•	•							H	H	39	H
Optometrists	•	•	•	•	•	•	•							H	H	8	H
Physicians	•	•	•	•	•	•	•						•	H	H	109	H
Podiatrists	•	•	•	•	•	•	•							H	H	4	H
Veterinarians	•	•	•	•	•	•	•	•	•					H	H	9	H

' Estimates not available.
² Less than 500.

Column key:

Job requirements: 1. Leadership/persuasion · 2. Helping/instructing others · 3. Problem-solving/creativity · 4. Initiative · 5. Work as part of a team · 6. Frequent public contact · 7. Manual dexterity · 8. Physical stamina · 9. Hazardous

Work environment: 10. Outdoors · 11. Confined · 12. Geographically concentrated · 13. Part-time

Occupational characteristics: 14. Earnings · 15. Employment growth · 16. Number of new jobs through 1995 (in thousands) · 17. Entry requirements

Occupation	1	2	3	4	5	6	7	8	9	10	11	12	13	14	15	16	17
Registered Nurses, Pharmacists, Dietitians, Therapists, and Physician Assistants																	
Dietitians and nutritionists	•	•	•	•	•	•								M	H	12	H
Occupational therapists	•	•	•	•	•	•	•	•						[1]	H	8	H
Pharmacists	•	•	•	•	•	•						•		H	L	15	H
Physical therapists	•	•	•	•	•	•	•	•						M	H	25	H
Physician assistants	•	•	•	•	•	•	•							M	H	10	M
Recreational therapists	•	•	•	•	•	•	•	•		•				M	H	4	M
Registered nurses	•	•	•	•	•	•	•	•	•				•	M	H	452	M
Respiratory therapists	•	•	•	•	•	•	•							M	H	11	L
Speech pathologists and audiologists	•	•	•	•	•	•								M	M	8	H
Health Technologists and Technicians																	
Clinical laboratory technologists and technicians		•		•		•					•			L	L	18	[2]
Dental hygienists		•		•	•	•	•						•	L	H	22	M
Dispensing opticians		•	•	•	•	•								M	H	10	M
Electrocardiograph technicians		•	•		•	•								[1]	M	3	M
Electroencephalographic technologists and technicians		•	•		•	•								[1]	H	1	M
Emergency medical technicians	•	•	•	•	•	•	•	•	•	•				L	L	3	M
Licensed practical nurses		•			•	•	•	•					•	L	M	106	M
Medical record technicians				•								•		L	H	10	M
Radiologic technologists		•			•	•	•		•					L	H	27	M
Surgical technicians		•			•	•	•							L	M	5	M
Writers, Artists, and Entertainers																	
Communications Occupations																	
Public relations specialists	•		•	•	•	•								H	H	30	H
Radio and television announcers and newscasters	•	•		•	•	•						•		L	M	6	H
Reporters and correspondents	•		•	•	•	•								[1]	M	13	H
Writers and editors	•		•	•	•							•	•	[1]	H	54	H
Visual Arts Occupations																	
Designers			•	•	•	•	•							H	H	46	H
Graphic and fine artists			•	•			•								H	60	M
Photographers and camera operators			•	•		•	•						•	M	H	29	M
Performing Arts Occupations																	
Actors, directors, and producers			•	•	•	•	•	•				•	•	L	H	11	M
Dancers and choreographers			•	•	•	•	•	•				•	•	L	H	2	M
Musicians			•	•	•	•	•	•				•	•	L	M	26	M

[1] Estimates not available.
[2] Vary, depending on job.

	Job requirements											Work environment		Occupational characteristics			
	1. Leadership/persuasion	2. Helping/instructing others	3. Problem-solving/creativity	4. Initiative	5. Work as part of a team	6. Frequent public contact	7. Manual dexterity	8. Physical stamina	9. Hazardous	10. Outdoors	11. Confined	12. Geographically concentrated	13. Part-time	14. Earnings	15. Employment growth	16. Number of new jobs through 1995 (in thousands)	17. Entry requirements
Technologists and Technicians Except Health																	
Engineering and Science Technicians																	
Drafters				●		●				●				M	M	39	M
Electrical and electronics technicians			●	●		●								M	H	202	M
Engineering technicians			●	●		●								M	H	90	M
Science technicians			●	●		●								M	M	40	M
Other technicians																	
Air traffic controllers	●	●	●	●		●				●				H	L	²	H
Broadcast technicians			●	●		●				●				M	H	5	M
Computer programmers			●	●						●				H	H	245	H
Legal assistants			¹	●	¹									M	H	51	L
Library technicians	●			●	●	●						●		L	L	4	L
Tool programmers, numerical control			●			●		●						M	H	3	M
Marketing and Sales Occupations																	
Cashiers		●			●	●				●		●	●	L	H	566	L
Insurance sales workers	●	●	●	●		●							●	M	L	34	M
Manufacturers' sales workers	●	●	●	●		●								H	L	51	H
Real estate agents and brokers	●	●	●	●		●				●		●		M	M	52	M
Retail sales workers	●	●	●	●		●						●		L	M	583	L
Securities and financial services sales workers	●	●	●	●		●						●		H	H	32	H
Travel agents	●	●	●	●		●								¹	H	32	M
Wholesale trade sales workers	●	●	●	●		●								M	H	369	M
Administrative Support Occupations, Including Clerical																	
Bank tellers					●	●				●			●	L	L	24	L
Bookkeepers and accounting clerks				●						●			●	L	L	118	L
Computer and peripheral equipment operators			●		●		●			●				L	H	143	M
Data entry keyers					●		●			●				L	L	10	L
Mail carriers					●	●	●		●					M	L	8	L
Postal clerks					●	●	●	●		●				M	L	−27	L
Receptionists and information clerks		●			●	●				●			●	L	M	83	L
Reservation and transportation ticket agents and travel clerks	●	●			●	●				●				M	L	7	L
Secretaries				●	●	●	●							L	L	268	L
Statistical clerks					●					●				L	L	−12	L
Stenographers				●	●	●	●							L	L	−96	L
Teacher aides	●	●			●	●	●	●					●	L	M	88	L
Telephone operators		●				●				●				L	M	89	L
Traffic, shipping, and receiving clerks			●	●	●									L	L	61	L
Typists						●				●			●	L	L	11	L

¹ Estimates not available.
² Less than 500.

Job requirements | Work environment | Occupational characteristics

Column key:
1. Leadership/persuasion
2. Helping/instructing others
3. Problem-solving/creativity
4. Initiative
5. Work as part of a team
6. Frequent public contact
7. Manual dexterity
8. Physical stamina
9. Hazardous
10. Outdoors
11. Confined
12. Geographically concentrated
13. Part-time
14. Earnings
15. Employment growth
16. Number of new jobs through 1995 (in thousands)
17. Entry requirements

	1	2	3	4	5	6	7	8	9	10	11	12	13	14	15	16	17
Service Occupations																	
Protective Service Occupations																	
Correction officers	●	●		●			●	●			●			M	H	45	L
Firefighting occupations		●	●		●	●	●	●	●	●			●	M	M	48	L
Guards						●	●	●	●		●		●	L	H	188	L
Police and detectives	●	●	●	●	●	●	●	●	●	●				M	M	66	L
Food and Beverage Preparation and Service Occupations																	
Bartenders			●		●	●			●				●	L	H	112	M
Chefs and cooks except short order			●			●	●		●				●	L	H	210	M
Waiters and waitresses			●		●	●	●						●	L	H	424	L
Health Service Occupations																	
Dental assistants		●			●	●	●	●					●	L	H	48	L
Medical assistants		●			●	●	●		●					L	H	79	L
Nursing aides		●			●	●	●	●	●				●	L	H	348	L
Psychiatric aides		●			●	●		●	●					L	L	5	L
Cleaning Service Occupations																	
Janitors and cleaners								●					●	L	M	443	L
Personal Service Occupations																	
Barbers					●	●	●				●		●	L	L	4	M
Childcare workers	●	●		●		●		●					●	L	L	55	L
Cosmetologists and related workers					●	●	●	●			●		●	L	H	150	M
Flight attendants		●			●	●	●	●						M	H	13	L
Agricultural, Forestry, and Fishing Occupations																	
Farm operators and managers	●	●	●	●	●			●	●		●			M	L	−62	L
Mechanics and Repairers																	
Vehicle and Mobile Equipment Mechanics and Repairers																	
Aircraft mechanics and engine specialists		●		●		●	●	●	●			●		H	M	18	M
Automotive and motorcycle mechanics		●			●	●	●	●			●			M	H	185	M
Automotive body repairers		●				●	●	●			●			M	M	32	M
Diesel mechanics		●			●	●	●	●			●			M	H	48	M
Farm equipment mechanics		●				●	●	●	●					M	L	2	M
Mobile heavy equipment mechanics		●				●	●	●			●			M	M	12	M

	1. Leadership/persuasion	2. Helping/instructing others	3. Problem-solving/creativity	4. Initiative	5. Work as part of a team	6. Frequent public contact	7. Manual dexterity	8. Physical stamina	9. Hazardous	10. Outdoors	11. Confined	12. Geographically concentrated	13. Part-time	14. Earnings	15. Employment growth	16. Number of new jobs 1995 (in thousands)	17. Entry requirements
Electrical and Electronic Equipment Repairers																	
Commercial and electronic equipment repairers		●	●		●	●								L	M	8	M
Communications equipment mechanics		●	●		●	●								M	L	3	M
Computer service technicians		●	●		●	●								M	H	28	M
Electronic home entertainment equipment repairers		●	●		●	●		●					●	M	M	7	M
Home appliance and power tool repairers		●	●		●	●								L	M	9	M
Line installers and cable splicers		●		●		●	●	●	●					M	M	24	L
Telephone installers and repairers		●		●	●	●	●	●						M	L	-19	L
Other Mechanics and Repairers																	
General maintenance mechanics		●				●		●						M	M	137	M
Heating, air-conditioning, and refrigeration mechanics		●				●		●						M	M	29	M
Industrial machinery repairers		●				●	●	●						M	L	34	M
Millwrights		●				●		●						H	L	6	M
Musical instrument repairers and tuners						●								L	L	1	M
Office machine and cash register servicers		●	●	●		●								M	H	16	M
Vending machine servicers and repairers		●	●			●								¹	M	5	M
Construction and Extractive Occupations																	
Construction Occupations																	
Bricklayers and stonemasons		●		●		●	●	●	●					M	M	15	M
Carpenters		●		●		●	●	●	●					M	M	101	M
Carpet installers		●		●	●	●	●	●						M	M	11	M
Concrete masons and terrazzo workers		●		●		●	●	●	●					M	M	17	M
Drywall workers and lathers		●		●		●	●	●						M	M	11	M
Electricians		●		●		●	●	●	●					H	M	88	M
Glaziers		●		●		●	●	●	●					M	H	8	M
Insulation workers		●		●		●	●	●						M	M	7	M
Painters and paperhangers		●		●	●	●	●	●						M	L	17	M
Plasterers		●		●		●	●	●				●		M	L	1	M
Plumbers and pipefitters		●		●	●	●	●	●	●					H	M	61	M
Roofers		●		●		●	●	●	●					L	M	16	M
Sheet-metal workers		●		●		●	●	●						M	M	16	M
Structural and reinforcing metal workers		●		●		●	●	●	●					H	M	16	M
Tilesetters		●		●		●	●							M	M	3	M
Extractive Occupations																	
Roustabouts				●		●	●	●	●			●		M	L	²	L

¹ Estimates not available.
² Less than 500.

	Job requirements									Work environment			Occupational characteristics				
	1. Leadership/persuasion	2. Helping/instructing others	3. Problem-solving/creativity	4. Initiative	5. Work as part of a team	6. Frequent public contact	7. Manual dexterity	8. Physical stamina	9. Hazardous	10. Outdoors	11. Confined	12. Geographically concentrated	13. Part-time	14. Earnings	15. Employment growth	16. Number of new jobs through 1995 (in thousands)	17. Entry requirements
Production Occupations																	
Blue-collar worker supervisors	•	•	•	•	•	•		•		•				M	L	85	M
Precision Production Occupations																	
Boilermakers		•				•		•						M	L	4	M
Bookbinding workers		•		•		•	•	•			•			L	M	14	M
Butchers and meatcutters						•	•	•	•		•			L	L	−9	M
Compositors and typesetters						•	•	•			•			L	M	14	M
Dental laboratory technicians							•				•			L	M	10	M
Jewelers	•	•	•	•	•	•	•				•	•		L	L	3	M
Lithographic and photoengraving workers		•	•		•	•	•				•			H	M	13	M
Machinists		•				•	•	•			•	•		M	L	37	M
Photographic process workers						•					•			L	H	14	L
Shoe and leather workers and repairers		•			•	•	•							L	L	−8	M
Tool-and-die makers		•				•	•	•			•	•		H	L	16	M
Upholsterers						•	•				•			L	L	6	M
Plant and System Operators																	
Stationary engineers		•				•	•	•			•			M	L	4	M
Water and sewage treatment plant operators		•	•			•			•	•	•			L	M	10	M
Machine Operators, Tenders, and Setup Workers																	
Metalworking and plastic-working machine operators						•	•	•			•	•			L	3	L
Numerical-control machine-tool operators		•				•	•	•			•			M	H	17	M
Printing press operators	•	•		•		•	•	•			•			M	M	26	M
Fabricators, Assemblers, and Handworking Occupations																	
Precision assemblers				•		•	•				•			L	M	66	L
Transportation equipment painters						•	•	•			•			M	M	9	M
Welders and cutters						•	•	•	•					M	M	41	M
Transportation and Material Moving Occupations																	
Aircraft pilots		•	•	•		•					•			H	H	18	M
Busdrivers			•		•	•	•				•		•	M	M	77	M
Construction machinery operators				•		•	•	•	•	•	•			M	M	32	M
Industrial truck and tractor operators			•			•	•				•			M	L	−46	M
Truckdrivers			•			•	•				•			M	M	428	M
Handlers, Equipment Cleaners, Helpers, and Laborers																	
Construction trades helpers				•		•	•	•	•					L	L	27	L

fying the motivational patterns associated with specific jobs and then fitting one's individual motivational pattern with the most appropriate jobs. For example, if a motivational pattern for a specific sales position with XYZ computer company is oriented toward (1) working with technical details, (2) operating in a structured environment where team work is important, and (3) using one's ability to plan, initiate new contacts, and follow-up, and your particular motivational pattern indicates that these are the subject matters, circumstances, abilities, and operating relationships central to your work behavior, then you may have an ideal "fit" with this particular job. While this technique does not use tests and checklists, it does require a great deal of content analysis of content analysis relevant to special positions. Ideally, this type of analysis should be done on positions within specific organizations. As such, it requires a great deal of investigative work for uncovering the right job for you.

COMPUTER PROGRAMS

Several computerized programs provide information on jobs and careers appropriate for people with particular skill and interest profiles. The most popular, comprehensive, and powerful programs are the *Discover II* and *Sigi-Plus*. Both programs assist users in identifying their skills and interests and then matching them with appropriate jobs. Both programs are widely used in career and counseling centers at community colleges as well as four-year colleges and universities. Even if you are not a student, you should be able to get access to these programs through your local community college. You might also check with your local high school, women's center, or library for information on the availability of these excellent assessment programs.

Several other computerized job matching programs are also available. In particular, look for the following:

- *Computerized Career Assessment and Planning Program*
- *Computerized Career Information System*
- *The Micro Guide to Careers Series*

CONDUCT RESEARCH

We strongly recommend that you conduct research on jobs and organizations related to your MAS and objectives. This research can take different forms, from consulting key directories and reading books on alternative jobs to interviewing employees and potential employers in particular organizations. Your goal should be to get as much detailed information on jobs and organizations as possible. You want to know how particular jobs and employers relate to your MAS and objectives:

- What types of people (personality, interests, skills) are best suited for each job?

- What type of environment do employees find themselves in?

- What appear to be the major requirements for success in this job?

- How are employees rewarded for their efforts?

- What kinds of relationships are employees expected to establish and maintain?

Answers to these questions will help you determine whether particular jobs and organizations are appropriate "fits" given your MAS and objectives.

Your local library should be filled with useful job and career information for initial research. Reference and document rooms of libraries have some of the best career resources. Career planning offices at colleges and universities have a wealth of job and career information in their specialized libraries—a wider selection than most general libraries.

You should start your research by examining several key directories that provide information on alternative jobs and careers:

- *The Occupational Outlook Handbook* (U.S. Department of Labor). This massive directory is the "bible" for identifying over 13,000 job titles. Each job is annotated, organized by major job categories, and cross-referenced by industry and title.

- *Occupational Outlook Handbook* (U.S. Department of Labor). Published biannually, this is the standard sourcebook on over 200 of America's most popular careers. Provides clear descriptions of each job, including working conditions, educational and training requirements, salaries, and future prospects.

- *Encyclopedia of Careers and Vocational Guidance*, 4 Volumes (J. G. Ferguson Co.). Newly revised (1990) this standard reference examines hundreds of technical and high-tech occupations in addition to the standard career and job fields. Vol 1: *Industry Profiles*; Vol. 2: *Professional Careers*; Vol. 3: *Specific and General Careers*; Vol. 4: *Technicians Careers*.

- *The Guide For Occupational Exploration* (National Forum Foundation). Based on the U.S. Department of Labor research, this guide lists more than 13,000 jobs by occupational cluster, skills required, job title, and industry groups. This is the key book that provides some analytical substance to the *Dictionary of Occupational Titles* and the *Occupational Outlook Handbook*.

You will also find several books that focus on alternative jobs and careers. National Textbook Company, for example, publishes one of the most comprehensive series of books on alternative jobs and careers. Their books now address 150+ different job and career fields. Representative titles in their *"Opportunities in..."* series include:

- *Opportunities in Advertising*
- *Opportunities in Airline Careers*
- *Opportunities in Banking*
- *Opportunities in Business Management*
- *Opportunities in Child Care*
- *Opportunities in Craft Careers*
- *Opportunities in Electrical Trades*

- *Opportunities in Eye Care*
- *Opportunities in Gerontology*
- *Opportunities in Interior Design*
- *Opportunities in Laser Technology*
- *Opportunities in Microelectronics*
- *Opportunities in Optometry*
- *Opportunities in Pharmacy*
- *Opportunities in Public Relations*
- *Opportunities in Robotics*
- *Opportunities in Sports and Athletics*
- *Opportunities in Telecommunications*
- *Opportunities in Word Processing*

They also publish another set of books in their *"Careers in..."* series:

- *Careers in Accounting*
- *Careers in Business*
- *Careers in Communications*
- *Careers in Computers*
- *Careers in Education*
- *Careers in Engineering*
- *Careers in Health Care*
- *Careers in Law*
- *Careers in Science*

Also look for ten volumes in the *"Career Advisory"* series published by Visible Ink Press (Gale Research):

- *Advertising Career Directory*
- *Book Publishing Career Directory*
- *Business and Finance Career Directory*
- *Health Care Career Directory*
- *Magazine Publishing Career Directory*
- *Marketing Career Directory*
- *Newspaper Publishing Career Directory*
- *Public Relations Career Directory*
- *Radio and Television Career Directory*
- *Travel and Hospitality Career Directory*

Walker and Company publishes a *"Career Choices"* series of books
closely linked to the subject majors of college students:

- *Career Choices: Art*
- *Career Choices: Business*
- *Career Choices: Communications and Journalism*
- *Career Choices: Computer Science*
- *Career Choices: Economics*
- *Career Choices: English*
- *Career Choices: History*
- *Career Choices: Law*
- *Career Choices: Mathematics*
- *Career Choices: MBA*
- *Career Choices: Political Science and Government*
- *Career Choices: Psychology*

Facts on File publishes seven books on alternative jobs and careers:

- *Career Opportunities in Advertising and Public Relations*
- *Career Opportunities in Art*
- *Career Opportunities in the Music Industry*
- *Career Opportunities in the Sports Industry*
- *Career Opportunities in Television, Cable, and Video*
- *Career Opportunities in Theater and Performing Arts*
- *Career Opportunities in Writing*

Many other books examine a wide range of jobs and careers.
Some are annual or biannual reviews of today's most popular jobs.
You should find several of these books particularly helpful:

- *100 Best Careers For the Year 2000*, Shelly Field (Prentice
  Hall/Arco)
- *100 Best Jobs For the 1990s and Beyond*, Carol Kleiman
  (Dearborn Financial)
- *101 Careers: A Guide to the Fastest-Growing Opportunities*,
  Michael Harkavy (Wiley)
- *American Almanac of Jobs and Salaries*, John W. Wright
  (Avon)
- *Best Jobs For the 1990s and Into the 21st Century*, Ron and
  Caryl Krannich (Impact Publications)

- *Careers Encyclopedia*, Craig Norback ed. (National Textbook)
- *Jobs 1993*, Ross and Kathryne Petras (Simon and Schuster)
- *Jobs! What They Are, Where They Are, What They Pay*, Robert and Anne Snelling (Simon and Schuster)
- *The Jobs Rated Almanac*, Les Krantz (Pharos Books)
- *New Emerging Careers*, S. Norman Feingold and Maxine H. Atwater (Garrett Park Press)
- *Top Professions*, Nicholas Basta (Peterson's)
- *Where the Jobs Are*, Alan Satterfield (Career Press)

Other books identify many of the best employers in today's job market:

- *Hoover's Handbook of American Business*, Gary, Campbell, and Spain (Reference Press)
- *Job Seeker's Guide to 1000 Top Employers*, Jennifer Arnold Mast (Visible Ink Press)
- *Job Seeker's Guide to Private and Public Companies* (Gale Research)

If you are unable to find these books in your local library or bookstore, they can be ordered directly from Impact Publications. Order information is found at the end of this book. You may also want to request a copy of their free catalog of over 1,400 annotated job and career resources which includes these titles.

CONTACT ORGANIZATIONS AND PEOPLE FOR INFORMATION

While examining directories and reading books on alternative jobs and careers will provide you with useful job search information, much of this material may be too general for specifying the right job for you. In the end, the best information will come directly from people in specific jobs in specific organizations. To get this information you must interview people.

You might begin your investigations by contacting various professional and trade associations for detailed information on jobs and careers relevant to their members. For names, addresses, and telephone numbers of such associations, consult the following key directories which are available in most libraries:

- *The Encyclopedia of Associations* (Gale Research)
- *National Trade and Professional Associations* (Columbia Books)

If you are interested in jobs with a particular organization, you should contact the personnel office for information on the types of jobs offered within the organization. You may be able to examine vacancy announcements which describe the duties and responsibilities of specific jobs. If you are interested in working for federal, state, or local governments, each agency will have a personnel office which can supply you with descriptions of their jobs. While gathering such information, be sure to ask people about their jobs.

Your most productive research activity will be talking to people. Informal, word-of-mouth communication is still the most effective channel of job search information. In contrast to reading books, people have more current, detailed, and accurate information. Ask them about:

- Occupational fields
- Job requirements and training
- Interpersonal environments
- Performance expectations
- Their problems
- Salaries
- Advancement opportunities
- Future growth potential of the organization
- How best to acquire more information and contacts in a particular field

You may be surprised how willingly friends, acquaintances, and strangers will give you useful information. But before you talk to people, do your library research so that you are better able to ask thoughtful questions.

NETWORK FOR INFORMATION, ADVICE, AND REFERRALS

As you get further into your job search, networking for information, advice, and referrals will become an important element in your overall job search strategy. At that time you will come into closer contact with potential employers who can provide you with detailed information on their organizations and specific jobs. If you have a well defined MAS, specific job objectives, and a well focused resume, you should be in a good position to make networking pay off with useful information, advice, and referrals. You will quickly discover that the process of linking your MAS and objectives to specific jobs is an ongoing one involving several steps in your job search.

Chapter Thirteen

USE TIME AND
PLAN EFFECTIVELY

Discovering the best job requires more than just thinking about what you want to do and completing a battery of self-assessment exercises and tests in the process of conducting a job or career change. You must go far beyond trying to understand who you are and what you want to do. At the very least you must use your time wisely and develop an effective plan of action that will direct your job search into fruitful areas that lead to job interviews and offers.

WHEN IN DOUBT, TAKE ACTION

The old adage *"When in doubt, do something"* is especially relevant when expanded to include a thoughtful plan of action related to the job search process as outlined in Chapter Four: *"When in doubt, engage in a concrete activity related to the sequence of job search steps."* This might include conducting research on communities, companies, positions, and salaries; surveying job vacancy announcements; writing a resume and job search letters; or contacting three employers each day.

But developing a plan and taking action is much easier said than done. If conducted properly, a job search can become an extremely time consuming activity. It inevitably competes with other personal and professional priorities. That's why you need to make some initial decisions as to how and when you will conduct a job search. How much time, for example, will you set aside each day or week to engage in each of the seven job search activities outlined in Chapter Four? After you've spent numerous hours identifying your abilities and skills and formulating an objective, are you willing to commit yourself to 20 hours a week to network for information and advice? If you are unwilling to commit both your time and yourself to each activity within the process, you may remain stuck, and inevitably frustrated, at the initial stages of self-awareness and understanding. Success only comes to those who take action at other stages in the job search process.

USE TIME WISELY

If you decide to conduct your own job search with minimum assistance from professionals, your major cost will be your time. Therefore, you must find sufficient time to devote to your job search. Ask yourself this question:

> "How valuable is my time in relation to
> finding a job or changing my career?"

Assign a dollar value to your time. For example, is your time worth $3, $5, $10, $25, $50, or $100 an hour? Compare your figure with what you might pay a professional for doing much of the job search work for you. Normal professional fees range from $2,000 to $12,000.

The time you devote to your job search will depend on whether you want to work at it on a full-time or part-time basis. If you are unemployed, by all means make this a full-time endeavor—40 to 80 hours per week. If you are presently employed, we do not recommend quitting your job in order to look for employment. You will probably need the steady income and attendant health benefits during your transition period. Furthermore, it is easier to find new employment by appearing employed. Unemployed people project a negative image in the eyes of many employers—they appear to need a job. **Your goal is to find a job based on your strengths rather than your needs.**

However, if you go back to school for skills retraining, your present employment status may be less relevant to employers. Your major strength is the fact that you have acquired a skill the employer needs. If you quit your job and spend money retraining, you will communicate a certain degree of risk-taking, drive, responsibility, and dedication which employers readily seek, but seldom find, in candidates today.

Assuming you will be conducting a job search on a part-time basis—15 to 25 hours per week—you will need to find the necessary time for these job activities. Unfortunately, most people are busy, having programmed every hour to "important" personal and professional activities. Thus, conducting a job search for 15 or more hours a week means that some things will have to go or receive low priority in relation to your job search.

This is easier said than done. The job search often gets low priority. It competes with other important daily routines, such as attending meetings, taking children to games, going shopping, and watching favorite TV programs. Rather than fight with your routines—and create family disharmony and stress—make your job search part of your daily routines by improving your overall management of time.

Certain time management techniques will help you make your job search a high priority activity in your daily schedule. These practices may actually lower your present stress level and thus enhance your overall effectiveness.

Time management experts estimate that most people waste their time on unimportant matters. Lacking priorities, people spend 80 percent of their time on trivia and 20 percent of their time on the important matters which should get most of their attention. If you reverse this emphasis, you could have a great deal of excess time—and probably experience less stress attendant with the common practice of crisis managing the critical 20 percent.

Before reorganizing your time, you must know how you normally use your time. Therefore, complete the following statement for a preliminary assessment of your time management behavior. While many of these statements especially pertain to individuals in managerial positions, respond to those statements that are most relevant to your employment situation.

YOUR TIME MANAGEMENT INVENTORY

Respond to each statement by circling "yes" or "no," depending on which response best represents your normal pattern of behavior.

1. I have a written set of long, intermediate, and short-range goals for myself (and my family).   Yes   No

2. I have a clear idea of what I will do today at work and at home.   Yes   No

3. I have a clear idea of what I want to accomplish at work this coming week and month.   Yes   No

4. I set priorities and follow-through on the most important tasks first.   Yes   No

5. I judge my success by the results I produce in relation to my goals.   Yes   No

6. I use a daily, weekly, and monthly calendar for scheduling appointments and setting work targets.   Yes   No

7. I delegate as much work as possible.   Yes   No

8. I get my subordinates to organize their time in relation to mine.   Yes   No

9. I file only those things which are essential to my work. When in doubt, I throw it out.   Yes   No

10. I throw away junk mail.   Yes   No

11. My briefcase is uncluttered, including only essential materials; it serves as my office away from the office.   Yes   No

12. I minimize the number of meetings and concentrate on making decisions rather than discussing aimlessly.   Yes   No

13. I make frequent use of the telephone and
face-to-face encounters rather than written
communications.   Yes   No

14. I make minor decisions quickly.   Yes   No

15. I concentrate on accomplishing one thing
at a time.   Yes   No

16. I handle each piece of paper once.   Yes   No

17. I answer most letters on the letter I receive.   Yes   No

18. I set deadlines for myself and others and
follow-through in meeting them.   Yes   No

19. I reserve time each week to plan.   Yes   No

20. My desk and work area are well organized
and clear.   Yes   No

21. I know how to say "no" and do so.   Yes   No

22. I first skim books, articles, and other
forms of written communication for ideas
before reading further.   Yes   No

23. I monitor my time use during the day by
asking myself *"How can I best use my time
at present?"*   Yes   No

24. I deal with the present by getting things
done that need to be done.   Yes   No

25. I maintain a time log to monitor the best
use of my time.   Yes   No

26. I place a dollar value on my time and
act accordingly.   Yes   No

27. My briefcase includes items I can work on
during spare time in waiting rooms, lines,
and airports.   Yes   No

28. I—not others—control my time.   Yes   No

29. I keep my door shut when I'm working.   Yes   No

30. I regularly evaluate to what degree I
    am achieving my stated goals.   Yes   No

If you answered "no" to many of these statements, you should consider incorporating a few basic time management principles and practices into your daily schedule.

Don't get to extremes by drastically restructuring your life around the "religion" of time management. If you followed all the advice of time management experts, you would probably alienate your family, friends, and colleagues with your narrow efficiency mentality!

A realistic time management approach is to start monitoring your time use and then gradually re-organize your time according to goals and priorities. This is all you need to do. Forget the elaborate flow charts that are the stuff of expensive time management workshops and consultants. Start by developing a time management log that helps you monitor your present use of time. Keep daily records of how you use your time over a two week period. Identify who controls your time and the results of your time utilization. Within two weeks, clear patterns will emerge. You may learn that you have an "open door" policy that enables others to control your time, leaving little time to do your own work. Based on this information, you may need to close your door and be more selective about access. You may find from your analysis that most of your time is used for activities that have few if any important outcomes. If this is the case, then you may need to set goals and prioritize daily activities.

A simple yet effective technique for improving your time management practices is to complete a "to do" list for each day. You can purchase tablets of these forms in many stationery and office supply stores, or you can develop your own "Things To Do Today" list. This list also should prioritize which activities are most important to accomplish each day. Include at the top of your list a particular job search activity or several activities that should be completed on each day. If you follow this simple time management practice, you will find the necessary time to include your job search in your daily routines. You can give your job search top priority. Better still, you will accomplish more in less time, and with better results.

PLAN TO TAKE ACTION

While we recommend that you plan your job search, we also caution you to avoid the excesses of too much planning. Like time management, planning should not be all-consuming. Planning makes sense because it requires that you set goals and develop strategies for achieving the goals. However, too much planning can blind you to unexpected occurrences and opportunities. Given the highly decentralized and chaotic nature of the job market, you want to do just enough planning so you will be in a position to take advantage of what will inevitably be unexpected occurrences and opportunities arising from your planned job search activities. Therefore, as you plan your job search, be sure you are flexible enough to take advantage of new opportunities.

Based on our discussion of the sequence of job search steps in Chapter Four (page 54), we outline on page 177 a hypothetical plan for conducting an effective job search. This plan incorporates the individual job search activities over a six month period. If you phase in the first five job search steps during the initial three to four weeks and continue the final four steps in subsequent weeks and months, you should begin receiving job offers within two to three months after initiating your job search. Interviews and job offers can come anytime—often unexpectedly—as you conduct your job search. An average time is three months, but it can occur within a week or take as long as five months. If you plan, prepare, and persist at the job search, the pay-off will be job interviews and offers.

While three months may seem a long time, especially if you have just lost your job and you need work immediately, you can shorten your job search time by increasing the frequency of your individual job search activities. If you are job hunting on a full-time basis, you may be able to cut your job search time in half. But don't expect to get a job—especially your best job—within a week or two. Job hunting requires time and hard work—perhaps the hardest work you will ever do—but if done properly, it pays off with a job that is right for you.

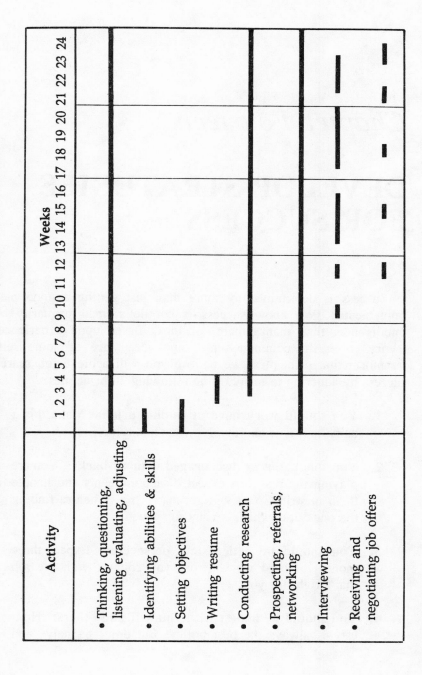

ORGANIZATION OF JOB SEARCH ACTIVITIES

Chapter Fourteen

DEVELOP STRATEGIES
FOR SUCCESS

Success is determined by more than just getting a good plan implemented. We know success is not determined primarily by intelligence, time management, or luck. Based upon experience, theory, research, common sense, and acceptance of some self-transformation principles, we believe you will achieve job search success by adhering to many of the following 20 principles:

1. **You should work hard at finding a job:** Make this a daily endeavor and involve your family.

2. **You should not be discouraged with set-backs:** You are playing the odds, so expect disappointments and handle them in stride. You will get many "no's" before finding the one "yes" which is right for you.

3. **You should be patient and persevere:** Expect three months of hard work before you connect with the job that's right for you.

4. **You should be honest with yourself and others:** Honesty is always the best policy. But don't be naive and

stupid by confessing your negatives and shortcomings to others.

5. **You should develop a positive attitude toward yourself:** Nobody wants to employ guilt-ridden people with inferiority complexes. Focus on your positive characteristics.

6. **You should associate with positive and successful people:** Finding a job largely depends on how well you relate to others. Avoid associating with negative and depressing people who complain and have a "you-can't-do-it" attitude. Run with winners who have a positive "can-do" outlook on life.

7. **You should set goals:** You should have a clear idea of what you want and where you are going. Without these, you will present a confusing and indecisive image to others. Clear goals help direct your job search into productive channels. Moreover, setting high goals will help make you work hard in getting what you want.

8. **You should plan:** Convert your goals into action steps that are organized as short, intermediate, and long-range plans.

9. **You should get organized:** Translate your plans into activities, targets, names, addresses, telephone numbers, and materials. Develop an efficient and effective filing system and use a large calendar for setting time targets and recording appointments and useful information.

10. **You should be a good communicator:** Take stock of your oral, written, and nonverbal communication skills. How well do you communicate? Since most aspects of your job search involve communicating with others, and communication skills are one of the most sought-after skills, always present yourself well both verbally and nonverbally.

11. **You should be energetic and enthusiastic:** Employers are attracted to positive people. They don't like negative and depressing people who toil at their work. Generate enthusiasm both verbally and nonverbally. Check on your telephone voice—it may be more unenthusiastic than your voice in face-to-face situations.

12. **You should ask questions:** Your best information comes from asking questions. Learn to develop intelligent questions that are non-aggressive, polite, and interesting to others. But don't ask too many questions.

13. **You should be a good listener:** Being a good listener is often more important than being a good questioner and talker. Learn to improve your face-to-face listening behavior (nonverbal cues) as well as remember and use information gained from others—if they need improving. Make others feel they enjoyed talking with you, i.e., you are one of the few people who actually **listens** to what they say.

14. **You should be polite, courteous, and thoughtful:** Treat gatekeepers, especially receptionists and secretaries, like human beings. Avoid being aggressive or too assertive. Try to be polite, courteous, and gracious. Your social graces are being observed. Remember to send thank-you letters—a very thoughtful thing to do in a job search. Even if rejected, thank employers for the "opportunity" given to you. After all, they may later have additional opportunities, and they will remember you.

15. **You should be tactful:** Watch what you say to others about other people and your background. Don't be a gossip, back-stabber, or confessor.

16. **You should maintain a professional stance:** Be neat in what you do and wear, and speak with the confidence, authority, and maturity of a professional.

17. **You should demonstrate your intelligence and competence:** Present yourself as someone who gets things done and achieves results—a **producer**. Employers generally seek people who are bright, hard working, responsible, communicate well, have positive personalities, maintain good interpersonal relations, are likable, observe dress and social codes, take initiative, are talented, possess expertise in particular areas, use good judgment, are cooperative, trustworthy, and loyal, generate confidence and credibility, and are conventional. In other words, they like people who score in the "excellent" to "outstanding" categories of the annual performance evaluation.

18. **You should not overdo your job search:** Don't engage in overkill and bore everyone with your "job search" stories. Achieve balance in everything you do. Occasionally take a few days off to do nothing related to your job search. Develop a system of incentives and rewards—such as two non-job search days a week, if you accomplish targets A, B, C, and D.

19. **You should be open-minded and keep an eye open for "luck":** Too much planning can blind you to unexpected and fruitful opportunities. You should welcome serendipity. Learn to re-evaluate your goals and strategies. Seize new opportunities if they appear appropriate.

20. **You should evaluate your progress and adjust:** Take two hours once every two weeks and evaluate what you are doing and accomplishing. If necessary, tinker with your plans and reorganize your activities and priorities. Don't become too routinized and thereby kill creativity and innovation.

These principles should provide you with an initial orientation for starting your job search. As you become more experienced, you will develop your own set of operating principles that should work for you in particular employment situations.

Chapter Fifteen

DISCOVER THE
RIGHT RESOURCES

Success in finding the best jobs also involves knowing which resources are the most useful for conducting a job search. While you chose this book as one of your resources, you should also discover many other resources that complement as well as extend this book into other critical job search steps.

Throughout this book we have mentioned several resources we feel will assist you at various stages in assessing your motivated abilities and skills, formulating a job objective, and identifying jobs appropriate for your particular mix of interests, values, abilities, skills, and objectives. Let's now turn to what we consider to be some of the best resources available for further expanding your job search beyond this book as we attempt to bring some coherence and organization to this literature to assist you in identifying any additional resources that might be useful to you in your job search.

Since many of these books cannot be found in local bookstores or libraries, you may need to order them directly from the publishers. For your convenience, you can order most of the books through Impact Publications by completing the order form at the end of this book. For a more complete listing of career planning and job search resources, contact our publisher to receive a free copy of their annotated catalog of over 1,400 career resources.

We mainly deal with books here, because they are the least expensive and most easily accessible resources in bookstores and libraries. However, more and more computer software programs are now available to assist you with two stages in your job search: self-assessment and resume writing. As mentioned in previous chapters, many career planning centers and some libraries and computer stores offer these resources.

CHOOSING WHAT'S BEST FOR YOU

During the past 20 years, hundreds of self-help books have been written on how to find a job and advance one's career. Each year dozens of additional volumes are published to inform as well as enlighten a growing audience of individuals concerned with conducting a proper job search.

You may be initially overwhelmed with the sheer volume of the career planning and job search literature available to help individuals find jobs and change careers. Once you examine a few books you will quickly learn that this literature is designed to be **used**. The books are not designed to describe or explain reality, develop a theory, nor predict the future.

Most career planning and job search books are designed to **advance self-help strategies** based upon the particular ideas or experiences of individual writers. They expound a **set of beliefs**— more or less logical and based on both experience and faith. Like other how-to literature on achieving success, you must first **believe** in these books before you can make them work for you. These books must be judged on the basis of faith and usefulness.

Given the nature of this literature, your best approach is to **pick and choose** which books are **more or less useful** for you. There is nothing magical about these books. At best, they may challenge your preconceptions; develop alternative beliefs which you may or may not find acceptable; provide you with some directions; and help motivate you to implement an effective job search. They will not get you a job.

The level of redundancy in this literature may disturb many readers. Moreso than in many other fields, career planning writers tend to quote each other or rely on the perspectives of a few key writers in restating the same approaches in a different form. As a result, many individuals confuse the high level of redundancy as repeated evidence of career and job "facts."

WHAT YOU GET

We have examined most of the career planning and job search literature with a view toward identifying the best of the lot. We've judged the literature in terms of its degree of accuracy, realism, comprehensiveness, and usefulness. In doing so, we have found four major types of books and some computer software which use different approaches to getting a job:

- **INFORMATION ON CAREER PLANNING AND JOB SEARCH SKILLS:** These resources include books on self-assessment, setting goals, conducting job research, writing resumes and job search letters, networking, interviewing, and negotiating salaries. Books with such titles as *Careering and Re-Careering For the 1990s, What Color Is Your Parachute?, Guerrilla Tactics in the New Job Market, The Complete Job Search Handbook, High Impact Resumes and Letters, Resumes That Knock 'Em Dead, Interview For Success, Sweaty Palms, Network Your Way to Job and Career Success,* and *Salary Success* are some of the most popular examples. The most popular computer software programs normally focus on assessing skills and producing resumes and cover letters. The most popular videos focus on the interview process.

- **INFORMATION ON SPECIFIC JOB AND CAREER FIELDS:** These resources are primarily directories and books surveying the basic job and career fields identified by the U.S. Department of Labor and published in their two major directories—*Dictionary of Occupational Titles* and *The Occupational Outlook Handbook.* Some publishers produce books similar to our general survey book of career fields with such titles as *100 Best Careers For the Year 2000* (Arco), *100 Best Jobs For the 1990s and Beyond* (Dearborn), *101 Careers* (Wiley), *Top Professions* (Peterson's), *The Jobs Rated Almanac* (Pharos Books), *New Emerging Careers* (Garrett Park Press), *Jobs 1993* (Simon and Schuster), and

Where the Jobs Are (Career Press). Numerous publishers have produced hundreds of books that address specific job and career fields outlined in these two directories. National Textbook, for example, produces nearly 180 specific career books with such titles as *Careers in Computers, Careers in High Tech, Careers in Mental Health, Opportunities in Aerospace, Opportunities in Carpentry, Opportunities in Laser Technology, Careers For Animal Lovers, Careers For Gourmets,* and *Careers For Numbers Crunchers*. Visible Ink Press (Gale Research in Detroit, MI) produces ten career directories with such titles as *Advertising Career Directory, Business and Finance Career Directory,* and *Travel and Hospitality Career Directory*. Facts on File publishes seven career directories with such titles as *Career Opportunities in Advertising and Public Relations, Career Opportunities in Sports Industry,* and *Career Opportunities in Writing*. Peterson's produces two popular annual directories: *Job Opportunities For Business and Liberal Arts Graduates* and *Job Opportunities For Engineering, Science, and Computer Graduates*. Some computer software programs also use the U.S. Department of Labor's data bases for assisting users in identifying jobs and careers best suited to their particular mix of interests, skills, and abilities. Two such popular programs are *The Occupational Outlook On Computer* and *EZ— D.O.T.*

- **INFORMATION ON SPECIFIC EMPLOYERS:** A few books and computer software programs attempt to identify the best employers for job seekers. These resources are either organized on a geographic basis—city and state employer directories—or by company. Two publishers dominate the geographic directories—Bob Adams, Inc. and Surrey Books— with such titles as *America's Fastest Growing Employers, National Job Bank, New York Job Bank, Atlanta Job Bank, How to Get a Job in San Francisco,* and *How to Get a Job in Boston*. Other publishers such as Ready Reference Press and the Visible Ink Press produce annual directories on employers: *Hoover's Handbook of American Business, Hoover's Handbook of World Business,* and *Job Seekers Guide to 1000 Top Employers*. One computer software program—*The JobHunt*—generates names and addresses of potential employers.

- **INFORMATION ON EMPLOYMENT GROUPS WITH SPECIAL NEEDS:** Primarily directories and books, these resources address the employment issues and needs facing special groups such as youth, women, minorities, unemployed, over 40 or 50 year old job seekers, relocating spouses, government employees, international groups, educators, temporary workers, telecommuters, high school graduates, military personnel, individuals with disabilities, and immigrants. Some of these books primarily address job search strategies unique for these groups or provide listings of associations, employment services, or potential employers responsive to the particular employment needs of these groups. Examples of such books include *Job Hunting For People With Disabilities, Directory of Special Programs For Minority Group Members, Minority Career Handbook, Work Sister Work, Congratulations You've Been Fired!, Smart Woman's Guide to Resumes and Job Hunting, Resumes For Re-Entry, Women's Job Search Handbook, Complete Guide to Public Employment, Find a Federal Job Fast!, Almanac of American Government Jobs and Careers, Complete Guide to International Jobs and Careers, Almanac of International Jobs and Careers, Guide to Careers in World Affairs, The New Relocating Spouse's Guide to Employment, Educator's Guide to Alternative Jobs and Careers, Retiring From the Military, Beyond the Uniform, Summer Opportunities For Kids and Teenagers, Getting a Job in the United States, 40+ Job Hunting Guide, Over 40 and Looking For Work?, Job Hunting After 50, Cracking the Over-50 Job Market, Temp Worker's Handbook,* and *Telecommuter's Handbook.*

BIBLIOGRAPHY

Best Jobs and Employers

Basta, Nicholas, *Top Professions: The 100 Most Popular, Dynamic, and Profitable Careers in America Today* (Princeton, NJ: Peterson's Guides, 1989).

Feingold, S. Norman and Maxine H. Atwater, *New Emerging Careers* (Garrett Park: Garrett Park Press, 1989).

Field, Shelly, *100 Best Careers For the Year 2000* (New York: Prentice Hall/Arco, 1992).

Gale Research, *Job Seeker's Guide to Private and Public Companies* (Detroit, MI: Gale Research, 1992).

Harkavy, Michael David, *101 Careers: A Guide to the Fastest-Growing Opportunities* (New York: Wiley & Sons, 1990).

Hoover, Gary, Alta Campbell, and Patrick J. Spain, *Hoover's Handbook of American Business* and *Hoover's Handbook of World Business* (Austin, TX: The Reference Press, 1993).

Kleiman, Carol, *The 100 Best Jobs For the 1990s and Beyond* (Chicago, IL: Dearborn Financial Publishing, 1992)

Krannich, Ronald L. and Caryl Rae, *The Best Jobs For 1990s and Into the 21st Century* (Manassas Park, VA: Impact Publications, 1993).

Krantz, Les, *The Jobs Rated Almanac* (New York: Pharos Books, 1992).

Mast, Jennifer Arnold, *The Job Seeker's Guide to 1000 Top Employers* (Detroit, MI: Visible Ink Press, 1993).

Petras, Kathryn and Ross, *Jobs '93* (New York: Simon & Schuster, 1993).

Satterfield, Alan, *Where the Jobs Are: The Hottest Careers For the '90s* (Hawthorne, NJ: Career Press, 1992).

Smith, Carter, *America's Fastest Growing Employers* (Holbrook, MA: Bob Adams, Inc., 1992).

Snelling, Robert O., Sr. and Anne M., *Jobs! What They Are, Where They Are, What They Pay!* (New York: Simon & Schuster, 1992).

Wright, John W. *American Almanac of Jobs and Salaries* (New York: Avon, 1990).

Job Search Strategies and Tactics

Elderkin, Kenton W., *How To Get Interviews From Classified Job Ads* (Manassas Park, VA: Impact Publications, 1993).

Figler, Howard E., *The Complete Job Search Handbook* (New York: Holt, Rinehart, and Winston, 1988).

Irish, Richard K., *Go Hire Yourself An Employer* (New York: Doubleday, 1987).

Jackson, Tom, *Guerrilla Tactics in the New Job Market* (New York: Bantam, 1993).

Kennedy, Joyce Lain and Darryl Laramore, *The Joyce Lain Kennedy's Career Book* (Lincolnwood, IL: National Textbook, 1992).

Krannich, Ronald L., *Careering and Re-Careering For the 1990s* (Manassas Park, VA: Impact Publications, 1993).

Krannich, Ronald L. and Caryl Rae, *Dynamite Tele-Search* (Manassas Park, VA: Impact Publications, 1993).

LaFevre, John L., *How You Really Get Hired* (New York: Prentice Hall, 1989).

Lathrop, Richard, *Who's Hiring Who* (Berkeley, CA: Ten Speed Press, 1989).

Lucht, John, *Rites of Passage At $100,000+* (New York: Viceroy Press, 1992)

McDonald, Scott A., *The Complete Job Finder's Guide For the 90's*, (Manassas Park, VA: Impact Publications, 1993).

Studner, Peter K., *Super Job Search* (Los Angeles, CA: Jamenair Ltd., 1989).

Wegmann, Robert and Robert Chapman, *The Right Place At the Right Time* (Berkeley, CA: Ten Speed Press, 1990).

Skills Identification, Testing, and Self-Assessment

Bolles, Richard N., *The New Quick Job Hunting Map* (Berkeley, CA: Ten Speed Press, 1990).

Bolles, Richard N., *The Three Boxes of Life* (Berkeley, CA: Ten Speed Press, 1981).

Bolles, Richard N., *What Color Is Your Parachute?* (Berkeley, CA: Ten Speed Press, 1993).

Crystal, John C. and Richard N. Bolles, *Where Do I Go From Here With My Life?* (Berkeley, CA: Ten Speed Press, 1979).

Gale, Barry and Linda Gale, *Discover What You're Best At* (New York: Simon & Schuster, 1990).

Holland, John L., *Making Vocational Choices* (Englewood Cliffs, NJ: Prentice-Hall, 1985).

Krannich, Ronald L. and Caryl Rae Krannich, *Discover the Best Jobs For You!* (Manassas Park, VA: Impact Publications, 1993).

Miller, Arthur F. and Ralph T. Mattson, *The Truth About You: Discover What You Should Be Doing With Your Life* (Berkeley, CA: Ten Speed Press, 1989).

Pilkington, Maya, *The Real-Life Aptitude Test* (New York: St. Martin's Press, 1989).

Sheele, Adele, *Skills For Success* (New York: Ballantine, 1979).

Sher, Barbara, *Wishcraft: How To Get What You Really Want* (New York: Ballantine, 1983).

Tieger, Paul D. and Barbara, *Do What You Are* (New York: Little, Brown, 1992).

Opportunities in Cities and States

Adams Inc., Bob (ed.), *The Job Bank Series: Atlanta, Boston, Chicago, Dallas, Denver, Detroit, Florida, Houston, Los Angeles, Minneapolis, New York, Ohio, Philadelphia, Phoenix, San Francisco, Seattle, St. Louis, Washington, DC* (Boston, MA: Bob Adams, Inc., 1992-1993).

Adams Inc., Bob (ed.), *The National Job Bank* (Boston, MA: Bob Adams, Inc., 1993).

Berreto, Helena, *California: Where To Work, Where To Live* (Rocklin, CA: Prima Publishing, 1989).

Camden, Bishop, Schwartz, Greene, Fleming-Holland, *"How To Get a Job in..." Insider's City Guides: Atlanta, Boston, Chicago, Houston, Dallas/Ft. Worth, New York, San Francisco, Seattle/Portland, Southern California, Washington, DC* (Chicago, IL: Surrey Books, 1990-1992).

Diefenbach, Greg and Phil Giordano, *Jobs in Washington, DC* (Manassas Park, VA: Impact Publications, 1992).

Alternative Jobs and Careers Fields

Angle, Susan and Alex Hiam, *Adventure Careers* (Hawthorne, NJ: Career Press, 1992).

Basta, Nicholas, *Environmental Career Guide* (New York: Wiley, 1991).

Career Associates, *Career Choices: Art, Business, Communications and Journalism, Computer Science, Economics, English, History, Law, Mathematics, MBA, Political Science and Government, Psychology* (New York: Walker and Co., 1990).

Career Associates, *Encyclopedia of Career Choices For the 1990s* (New York: Putnam, 1991).

Damp, Dennis V., *Health Career Job Explosion* (Coraopolis, PA: D-Amp Publications, 1993).

Morgan, Bradley, J. (ed.), *The Career Advisory Series: Advertising, Book Publishing, Business and Finance, Healthcare, Magazine Publishing, Marketing and Sales, Newspaper Publishing, Public Relations, Radio and Television, Travel and Hospitality* (Detroit, MI: Visible Ink Press, 1992-1993).

Harrington, Thomas F. and Arthur J. O'Shea (eds.), *Guide For Occupational Exploration* (Circle Pines, MN: American Guidance Service, 1989).

Hopke, William (ed.), *Encyclopedia of Careers and Vocational Guidance* (Chicago, IL: J. G. Ferguson, 1990).

National Textbook, *"Opportunities in..." Series*. 160+ titles on different career fields, such as Banking, Crafts, Energy, Engineering, Gerontology, Nursing, Psychiatry, Sports Medicine, and Travel (Lincolnwood, IL: National Textbook Co., 1984-1993).

National Textbook, *"Careers in..." Career Guidance Series*. 13 books on *Accounting, Advertising, Business, Communications, Computers, Education, Engineering, Health Care, High Tech, Law, Marketing, Medicine, Science* (Lincolnwood, IL: National Textbook Co., 1990-1993).

Norback, Craig T., *Careers Encyclopedia* (Lincolnwood, IL: National Textbook, 1992).

Peterson's, *Job Opportunities For Business and Liberal Arts Graduates* (Princeton, NJ: Peterson's Guides, 1993).

Peterson's, *Job Opportunities For Engineering, Science, and Computer Graduates* (Princeton, NJ: Peterson's Guides, 1993).

Rubin, K., *Flying High in Travel* (New York: Wiley, 1992).

Schwartz, Lester and Irv Brechner, *The Career Finder* (New York: Ballantine, 1990).

Shenk, Ellen, *Outdoor Careers* (Harrisburg, PA: Stackpole Books, 1992).

Stienstra, Tom, *Careers in the Outdoors* (San Francisco, CA: Foghorn Press, 1992).

U.S. Department of Labor, *Dictionary of Occupational Titles* (Washington, DC: Department of Labor, 1991).

U.S. Department of Labor, *Occupational Outlook Handbook* (Washington, DC: Department of Labor, 1992).

Resumes and Letters

Asher, Donald, *The Overnight Resume* (Berkeley, CA: Ten Speed Press, 1991).

Beatty, Richard H., *The Perfect Cover Letter* (New York: Wiley, 1989).

Bostwick, Burdette E., *Resume Writing* (New York: Wiley, 1992).

Cohen, Hiyaguha, *The No-Pain Resume Book* (Homewood, IL: Business One Irwin, 1992).

Frank, William S., *200 Letters For Job Hunters* (Berkeley, CA: Ten Speed Press, 1990).

Fry, Ronald W., *Your First Resume* (Hawthorne, NJ: Career Press, 1991).

Good, C. Edward, *Does Your Resume Wear Blue Jeans?* (Charlottesville, VA: Blue Jeans Press, 1985).

Jackson, Tom, *The Perfect Resume* (New York: Doubleday, 1990).

Kaplan, Robbie Miller, *Sure-Hire Resumes* (New York: AMACOM, 1990).

Krannich, Ronald L. and Caryl Rae Krannich, *Dynamite Cover Letters* (Manassas Park, VA: Impact Publications, 1992).

Krannich, Ronald L. and Caryl Rae Krannich, *Dynamite Resumes* (Manassas Park, VA: Impact Publications, 1992).

Krannich, Ronald L. and William J. Banis, *High Impact Resumes and Letters* (Manassas Park, VA: Impact Publications, 1992).

Krannich, Ronald L. and Caryl Rae Krannich, *Job Search Letters That Get Results* (Manassas Park, VA: Impact Publications, 1992).

Parker, Yana, *The Damn Good Resume Guide* (Berkeley, CA: Ten Speed Press, 1986).

Parker, Yana, *The Resume Catalog* (Berkeley, CA: Ten Speed Press, 1988).

Schuman, Nancy and William Lewis, *Revising Your Resume* (New York: Wiley, 1987).

Swanson, David, *The Resume Solution* (Indianapolis, IN: JIST Works, 1990).

Yate, John, *Cover Letters That Knock 'Em Dead* (Holbrook, MA: Bob Adams, 1992).

Yate, John, *Resumes That Knock 'Em Dead* (Holbrook, MA: Bob Adams, 1988).

Networking

Baber, Anne and Lynne Waymon, *Great Connections: Small Talk and Networking For Businesspeople* (Manassas Park, VA: Impact Publications, 1992).

Boe, Anne and Bettie B. Youngs, *Is Your "Net" Working?* (New York: Wiley, 1989).

Krannich, Ronald L. and Caryl Rae Krannich, *The New Network Your Way To Job and Career Success* (Manassas Park, VA: Impact Publications, 1993).

Raye-Johnson, Venda, *Effective Networking* (Palo Alto, CA: Crisp Publications, 1990).

Roane, Susan, *How To Work a Room* (New York: Warner Books, 1989).

Vilas, Donna and Sandy, *Power Networking* (Austin, TX: Mountain-Harbour Publications, 1992).

Dress, Appearance, and Image

Bixler, Susan, *The Professional Image* (New York: Putnam, 1984).

Bixler, Susan, *Professional Presence* (New York: Putnam, 1991).

Jackson, Carole, *Color Me Beautiful* (Washington, DC: Acropolis, 1986).

Molloy, John T., *John Molloy's New Dress For Success* (New York: Warner, 1989).

Molloy, John T., *The Woman's Dress For Success Book* (New York: Warner, 1977).

Nicholson, JoAnne and Judy Lewis-Crum, *Color Wonderful* (New York: Bantam, 1986).

Stran, Pamela Redmond, *Dressing Smart* (New York: Doubleday, 1990).

Interviews and Salary Negotiations

Beatty, R. H., *The Five Minute Interview* (New York: Wiley, 1986).

Chapman, Jack, *How To Make $1000 A Minute: Negotiating Salaries and Raises* (Berkeley, CA: Ten Speed Press, 1987).

Drake, John D., *The Perfect Interview* (New York, AMACOM, 1991).

Krannich, Caryl Rae and Ronald L. Krannich, *Dynamite Answers To Interview Questions: No More Sweaty Palms!* (Manassas Park, VA: Impact Publications, 1992).

Krannich, Caryl Rae and Ronald L. Krannich, *Interview For Success* (Manassas Park, VA: Impact Publications, 1993).

Krannich, Ronald L. and Caryl Rae Krannich, *Salary Success* (Manassas Park, VA: Impact Publications, 1990).

Medley, H. Anthony, *Sweaty Palms* (Berkeley, CA: Ten Speed Press, 1991).

Yeager, Neil and Lee Hough, *Power Interviews* (New York: Wiley, 1990).

Educators

Bastress, Frances, *Teachers In New Careers* (Cranston, RI: Carroll Press, 1984).

Krannich, Ronald L., *The Educator's Guide To Alternative Jobs and Careers* (Manassas Park, VA: Impact Publications, 1991).

Pollack, Sandy, *Alternative Careers For Teachers* (Boston, MA: Harvard Common Press, 1986).

Public-Oriented Careers

Krannich, Ronald L. and Caryl Rae Krannich, *The Almanac of American Government Jobs and Careers* (Manassas Park, VA: Impact Publications, 1991).

Krannich, Ronald L. and Caryl Rae Krannich, *The Complete Guide To Public Employment* (Manassas Park, VA: Impact Publications, 1990).

Krannich, Ronald L. and Caryl Rae Krannich, *Find a Federal Job Fast!* (Manassas Park, VA: Impact Publications, 1992).

Lauber, Daniel, *The Government Job Finder* (River Forest, IL: Planning/Communications, 1992).

Lauber, Daniel, *The Nonprofit's Job Finder* (River Forest, IL: Planning/Communications, 1992).

Lewis, William and Carol Milano, *Profitable Careers in Nonprofit* (New York: Wiley, 1987).

Smith, Devon Cottrell (ed.), *Great Careers: The Fourth of July Guide To Careers, Internships, and Volunteer Opportunities in the Nonprofit Sector* (Garrett Park, MD: Garrett Park Press, 1990).

Waelde, David E., *How To Get a Federal Job* (Washington, DC: FEDHELP, 1989).

Wood, Patricia, *The 171 Reference Book* (Washington, DC: Workbooks, Inc., 1991).

International and Overseas Jobs

Beckmann, David M., Timothy J. Mitchell, and Linda L. Powers, *The Overseas List* (Minneapolis, MN: Augsburg Publishing, 1986).

Foreign Policy Association (ed.), *Guide To Careers in World Affairs* (Manassas Park, VA: Impact Publications, 1993).

Kocher, Eric, *International Jobs* (Reading, MA: Addison-Wesley, 1989).

Krannich, Ronald L. and Caryl Rae Krannich, *The Almanac of International Jobs and Careers* (Manassas Park, VA: Impact Publications, 1991).

Krannich, Ronald L. and Caryl Rae Krannich, *The Complete Guide To International Jobs and Careers* (Manassas Park, VA: Impact Publications, 1992).

Krannich, Ronald L. and Caryl Rae Krannich, *Jobs For People Who Love Travel* (Manassas Park, VA: Impact Publications, 1993).

Sanborn, Robert, *How To Get a Job in Europe* (Chicago, IL: Surrey Books, 1990).

Sanborn, Robert, *How To Get a Job in the Pacific Rim* (Chicago, IL: Surrey Books, 1992).

Win, David, *International Careers: An Insider's Guide* (Charlotte, VT: Williamson Publishing, 1987).

Military

Bradley, Jeff, *A Young Person's Guide To the Military* (Boston, MA: Harvard Common Press, 1987).

Fitzpatrick, William G. and C. Edward Good, *Does Your Resume Wear Combat Boots?* (Charlottesville, VA: Blue Jeans Press, 1990).

Henderson, David G., *Job Search: Marketing Your Military Experience in the 1990s* (Harrisburg, PA: Stackpole Books, 1991).

Jacobsen, Kenneth C., *Retiring From the Military* (Annapolis, MD: Naval Institute Press, 1990).

Marrs, Texe and Karen Read, *The Woman's Guide To Military Service* (Cockeysville, MD: Liberty Publishing, 1986).

CAREER RESOURCES

Contact Impact Publications to receive a free copy of their latest comprehensive and annotated catalog of over 1,400 career resources (books, subscriptions, training programs, videos, audiocassettes, computer software).

The following career resources, many of which are mentioned in previous chapters, are available directly from Impact Publications. Complete the following form or list the titles, include postage (see formula at the end), enclose payment, and send your order to:

IMPACT PUBLICATIONS
9104-N Manassas Drive
Manassas Park, VA 22111
Tel. 703/361-7300
FAX 703/335-9486

Orders from individuals must be prepaid by check, moneyorder, Visa or MasterCard number. We accept telephone and FAX orders with a Visa or MasterCard number.

Qty.	TITLES	Price	TOTAL

BEST JOBS AND EMPLOYERS FOR THE 90s

Qty.	TITLES	Price	TOTAL
___	100 Best Careers For the Year 2000	$14.95	_____
___	100 Best Jobs For the 1990s and Beyond	$19.95	_____
___	101 Careers	$12.95	_____
___	American Almanac of Jobs and Salaries	$15.95	_____
___	America's 50 Fastest Growing Jobs	$9.95	_____
___	America's Fastest Growing Employers	$14.95	_____
___	Best Jobs For the 1990s and Into the 21st Century	$12.95	_____
___	Hoover's Handbook of American Business (annual)	$24.95	_____
___	Hoover's Handbook of World Business (annual)	$21.95	_____
___	Job Seeker's Guide To 1000 Top Employers	$22.95	_____
___	Jobs! What They Are, Where They Are, What They Pay	$13.95	_____
___	Jobs 1993	$15.95	_____
___	Jobs Rated Almanac	$15.95	_____
___	New Emerging Careers	$14.95	_____
___	Top Professions	$10.95	_____
___	Where the Jobs Are	$9.95	_____

KEY DIRECTORIES

___ Career Training Sourcebook	$24.95	___
___ Careers Encyclopedia	$39.95	___
___ Dictionary of Occupational Titles	$39.95	___
___ Directory of Executive Recruiters (annual)	$39.95	___
___ Directory of Outplacement Firms	$74.95	___
___ Directory of Special Programs For Minority Group Members	$31.95	___
___ Encyclopedia of Careers and Vocational Guidance	$129.95	___
___ Enhanced Guide For Occupational Exploration	$29.95	___
___ Government Directory of Addresses and Telephone Numbers	$79.95	___
___ Internships (annual)	$28.95	___
___ Job Bank Guide To Employment Services (annual)	$149.95	___
___ Job Hunter's Sourcebook	$49.95	___
___ Moving and Relocation Directory	$125.00	___
___ National Directory of Addresses & Telephone Numbers	$89.95	___
___ National Job Bank (annual)	$229.95	___
___ National Trade and Professional Associations	$69.95	___
___ Minority Organizations	$50.00	___
___ Occupational Outlook Handbook	$22.95	___
___ Professional Careers Sourcebook	$79.95	___

JOB SEARCH STRATEGIES AND TACTICS

___ But What If I Don't Want To Go To College	$10.95	___
___ Career Planning and Development For College Students and Recent Graduates	$17.95	___
___ Careering and Re-Careering For the 1990s	$13.95	___
___ Complete Job Search Handbook	$12.95	___
___ Dynamite Tele-Search	$10.95	___
___ Get the Right Job in 60 Days or Less	$12.95	___
___ Go Hire Yourself an Employer	$9.95	___
___ Guerrilla Tactics in the New Job Market	$11.95	___
___ How To Get Interviews From Classified Job Ads	$14.95	___
___ Joyce Lain Kennedy's Career Book	$29.95	___
___ Knock 'Em Dead	$19.95	___
___ Perfect Job Search	$12.95	___
___ Professional's Job Finder	$15.95	___
___ Right Place At the Right Time	$11.95	___
___ Rites of Passage At $100,000+	$29.95	___
___ Super Job Search	$22.95	___
___ Take Charge of Your Career	$10.95	___
___ Who's Hiring Who	$9.95	___
___ Work in the New Economy	$14.95	___

CITY AND STATE JOB FINDERS

___ California: Where To Work, Where To Live	$9.95	___
___ Jobs in Washington, DC	$11.95	___
___ L.A. Job Market Handbook	$15.95	___

How To Get a Job In . . .

___ Atlanta	$15.95	_____
___ Boston	$15.95	_____
___ Chicago	$15.95	_____
___ Dallas/Fort Worth	$15.95	_____
___ Houston	$15.95	_____
___ New York	$15.95	_____
___ San Francisco	$15.95	_____
___ Seattle/Portland	$15.95	_____
___ Southern California	$15.95	_____
___ Washington, DC	$15.95	_____

Bob Adams' Job Banks to:

___ Atlanta	$15.95	_____
___ Boston	$15.95	_____
___ Chicago	$15.95	_____
___ Dallas/Fort Worth	$15.95	_____
___ Denver	$15.95	_____
___ Detroit	$15.95	_____
___ Florida	$15.95	_____
___ Houston	$15.95	_____
___ Los Angeles	$15.95	_____
___ Minneapolis	$15.95	_____
___ New York	$15.95	_____
___ Ohio	$15.95	_____
___ Philadelphia	$15.95	_____
___ Phoenix	$15.95	_____
___ San Francisco	$15.95	_____
___ Seattle	$15.95	_____
___ Washington, DC	$15.95	_____

ALTERNATIVE JOBS AND CAREERS

___ Adventure Careers	$9.95	_____
___ Advertising Career Directory	$17.95	_____
___ Book Publishing Career Directory	$17.95	_____
___ Business and Finance Career Directory	$17.95	_____
___ But What If I Don't Want To Go To College?	$10.95	_____
___ Career Opportunities in Advertising and Public Relations	$27.95	_____
___ Career Opportunities in Art	$27.95	_____
___ Career Opportunities in the Music Industry	$27.95	_____
___ Career Opportunities in the Sports Industry	$27.95	_____
___ Career Opportunities in TV, Cable, and Video	$27.95	_____
___ Career Opportunities in Theater and Performing Arts	$27.95	_____
___ Career Opportunities in Writing	$27.95	_____
___ Careers For Animal Lovers	$12.95	_____
___ Careers For Bookworms	$12.95	_____
___ Careers For Foreign Language Speakers	$12.95	_____
___ Careers For Good Samaritans	$12.95	_____
___ Careers For Gourmets	$12.95	_____
___ Careers For Nature Lovers	$12.95	_____

___ Careers For Numbers Crunchers	$12.95	_____
___ Careers For Sports Nuts	$12.95	_____
___ Careers For Travel Buffs	$12.95	_____
___ Careers in Computers	$16.95	_____
___ Careers in Education	$16.95	_____
___ Careers in Health Care	$16.95	_____
___ Careers in High Tech	$16.95	_____
___ Careers in Law	$16.95	_____
___ Careers in Medicine	$16.95	_____
___ Careers in Mental Health	$10.95	_____
___ Careers in the Outdoors	$12.95	_____
___ Encyclopedia of Career Choices For the 1990s	$19.95	_____
___ Environmental Career Guide	$14.95	_____
___ Environmental Jobs For Scientists and Engineers	$14.95	_____
___ Health Care Job Explosion	$14.95	_____
___ Healthcare Career Directory	$17.95	_____
___ Magazine Publishing Career Directory	$17.95	_____
___ Marketing and Sales Career Directory	$17.95	_____
___ Newspaper Publishing Career Directory	$17.95	_____
___ Opportunities in Accounting	$13.95	_____
___ Opportunities in Advertising	$13.95	_____
___ Opportunities in Beauty Culture	$13.95	_____
___ Opportunities in Biological Sciences	$13.95	_____
___ Opportunities in Chemistry	$13.95	_____
___ Opportunities in Civil Engineering	$13.95	_____
___ Opportunities in Computer Science	$13.95	_____
___ Opportunities in Counseling & Development	$13.95	_____
___ Opportunities in Dental Care	$13.95	_____
___ Opportunities in Electronic & Electrical Engineering	$13.95	_____
___ Opportunities in Environmental Careers	$13.95	_____
___ Opportunities in Financial Career	$13.95	_____
___ Opportunities in Fitness	$13.95	_____
___ Opportunities in Gerontology	$13.95	_____
___ Opportunities in Health & Medical Careers	$13.95	_____
___ Opportunities in Journalism	$13.95	_____
___ Opportunities in Laser Technology	$13.95	_____
___ Opportunities in Law	$13.95	_____
___ Opportunities in Marketing	$13.95	_____
___ Opportunities in Medical Technology	$13.95	_____
___ Opportunities in Microelectronics	$13.95	_____
___ Opportunities in Nursing	$13.95	_____
___ Opportunities in Paralegal Careers	$13.95	_____
___ Opportunities in Pharmacy	$13.95	_____
___ Opportunities in Psychology	$13.95	_____
___ Opportunities in Teaching	$13.95	_____
___ Opportunities in Telecommunications	$13.95	_____
___ Opportunities in Television & Video	$13.95	_____
___ Opportunities in Veterinary Medicine	$13.95	_____
___ Opportunities in Waste Management	$13.95	_____
___ Outdoor Careers	$14.95	_____
___ Public Relations Career Directory	$17.95	_____
___ Radio and Television Career Directory	$17.95	_____
___ Travel and Hospitality Career Directory	$17.95	_____

INTERNATIONAL AND OVERSEAS JOBS

___ Almanac of International Jobs and Careers	$14.95 ___
___ Building an Import/Export Business	$14.95 ___
___ Complete Guide To International Jobs & Careers	$13.95 ___
___ Directory of Jobs and Careers Abroad	$14.95 ___
___ Directory of Overseas Summer Jobs	$14.95 ___
___ Getting Your Job in the Middle East	$19.95 ___
___ Guide To Careers in World Affairs	$13.95 ___
___ How To Get a Job in Europe	$17.95 ___
___ How To Get a Job in the Pacific Rim	$17.95 ___
___ How To Get a Job With a Cruise Line	$12.95 ___
___ International Consultant	$22.95 ___
___ International Directory of Voluntary Work	$13.95 ___
___ International Jobs	$12.95 ___
___ Job Hunter's Guide To Japan	$12.95 ___
___ Jobs For People Who Love Travel	$12.95 ___
___ Jobs in Paradise	$11.95 ___
___ Teaching English Abroad	$13.95 ___
___ Work, Study, Travel Abroad	$16.95 ___

GOVERNMENT AND PUBLIC-ORIENTED CAREERS

___ The 171 Reference Book	$18.95 ___
___ Almanac of American Government Jobs and Careers	$14.95 ___
___ Book of $16,000-$60,000 Post Office Jobs	$14.95 ___
___ Book of U.S. Government Jobs	$15.95 ___
___ Complete Guide To Public Employment	$15.95 ___
___ Federal Jobs For College Graduates	$14.95 ___
___ Federal Jobs in Law Enforcement	$15.95 ___
___ Find a Federal Job Fast!	$9.95 ___
___ Government Job Finder	$14.95 ___
___ Paralegal	$10.95 ___

NONPROFIT CAREERS

___ Good Works	$18.00 ___
___ Great Careers	$36.00 ___
___ Non-Profits' Job Finder	$14.95 ___
___ Profitable Careers in Nonprofits	$14.95 ___

COMPUTER SOFTWARE

___ Computerized Career Assessment & Planning Program	$489.95 ___
___ Computerized Career Information System	$309.95 ___
___ EZ—D.O.T.	$299.95 ___
___ JOBHUNT Quick and Easy Employer Contacts	$49.95 ___
___ INSTANT Job Hunting Letters	$39.95 ___
___ Occupational Outlook on Computer	$129.95 ___
___ Perfect Resume Computer Kit (Personal)	$49.95 ___
___ Quick and Easy 171's (Individual)	$49.95 ___
___ ResumeMaker	$49.95 ___

VIDEOS

___ Find the Job You Want...and Get It! (4 videos)	$229.95	_____
___ How To Present a Professional Image (2 videos)	$149.95	_____
___ Insider's Guide To Competitive Interviewing	$49.95	_____
___ Networking Your Way To Success	$79.95	_____
___ Winning At Job Hunting in the 90s	$89.95	_____

JOB LISTINGS AND VACANCY ANNOUNCEMENTS

___ Federal Career Opportunities (6 biweekly issues)	$38.00	_____
___ International Employment Gazette (6 biweekly issues)	$35.00	_____

SKILLS, TESTING, SELF-ASSESSMENT

___ Career Exploration Inventory	$24.95	_____
___ Career Sort Assessment Instruments	$27.95	_____
___ Discover the Best Jobs For You!	$11.95	_____
___ Do What You Are	$14.95	_____
___ New Quick Job Hunting Map	$3.95	_____
___ Test Your I.Q.	$6.95	_____
___ Three Boxes of Life	$14.95	_____
___ Truth About You	$11.95	_____
___ What Color Is Your Parachute?	$14.95	_____
___ Where Do I Go From Here With My Life?	$10.95	_____
___ Wishcraft	$9.95	_____

EMPOWERMENT, SELF-ESTEEM, MANAGING CHANGE

___ 7 Habits of Highly Effective People	$11.00	_____
___ Bouncing Back	$14.95	_____
___ Courage To Fail	$18.95	_____
___ Do What You Love, the Money Will Follow	$8.95	_____
___ Dreams That Can Change Your Life	$18.95	_____
___ Softpower	$10.95	_____
___ Staying Up When Your Job Pulls You Down	$10.95	_____
___ Work With Passion	$9.95	_____
___ Your Own Worst Enemy	$19.95	_____

RESUMES, LETTERS, NETWORKING

___ Dynamite Cover Letters	$9.95	_____
___ Dynamite Resumes	$9.95	_____
___ Encyclopedia of Job-Winning Resumes	$16.95	_____
___ Great Connections	$11.95	_____
___ High Impact Resumes and Letters	$12.95	_____
___ How To Work a Room	$9.95	_____
___ Job Search Letters That Get Results	$12.95	_____
___ New Network Your Way To Job and Career Success	$11.95	_____
___ No-Pain Resume Book	$14.95	_____
___ Perfect Cover Letter	$9.95	_____
___ Perfect Resume	$12.00	_____

___ Perfect Resume Strategies $12.50 _____
___ Power Networking $12.95 _____
___ Power Resumes $12.95 _____
___ Resume Catalog $15.95 _____
___ Resumes For High School Graduates $9.95 _____
___ Revising Your Resume $13.95 _____
___ Smart Woman's Guide To Resumes
and Job Hunting $8.95 _____
___ Sure-Hire Resumes $14.95 _____
___ Your First Resume $10.95 _____

DRESS, APPEARANCE, IMAGE, ETIQUETTE

___ Dressing Smart $19.95 _____
___ John Molloy's New Dress For Success $10.95 _____
___ Professional Presence $21.95 _____

INTERVIEWS AND SALARY NEGOTIATIONS

___ Dynamite Answers To Interview Questions $9.95 _____
___ Interview For Success $11.95 _____
___ Listening: The Forgotten Skill $12.95 _____
___ Perfect Follow-Up Method To Win the Job $9.95 _____
___ Perfect Interview $17.95 _____
___ Power Interviews $12.95 _____
___ Salary Success $11.95 _____
___ Sweaty Palms $9.95 _____

MILITARY

___ Beyond the Uniform $12.95 _____
___ Civilian Career Guide $12.95 _____
___ Does Your Resume Wear Combat Boots? $9.95 _____
___ Job Search: Marketing Your Military Experience $14.95 _____
___ Re-Entry $13.95 _____
___ Retiring From the Military $22.95 _____
___ Woman's Guide To Military Service $9.95 _____
___ Young Person's Guide To the Military $9.95 _____

WOMEN AND SPOUSES

___ New Relocating Spouse's Guide To Employment $14.95 _____
___ Resumes For Re-Entry: A Handbook For Women $10.95 _____
___ Smart Woman's Guide To Resumes and Job Hunting $8.95 _____
___ Women's Job Search Handbook $12.95 _____

MINORITIES AND DISABLED

___ Directory of Special Programs For
Minority Group Members $31.95 _____
___ Job Hunting For People With Disabilities $14.95 _____
___ Minority Organizations $49.95 _____

___ Work, Sister, Work $16.95 _____

COLLEGE STUDENTS

___ College Majors and Careers $15.95 _____
___ Complete Resume and Job Search Book
      For College Students $9.95 _____
___ Graduating To the 9-5 World $11.95 _____
___ Liberal Arts Jobs $10.95 _____
___ MBA'S Guide To Career Planning $16.95 _____

UNIQUE JOB SEARCH SERVICES
(see page 213 for descriptions)

___ Job Bank USA Enrollment $30.00 _____
___ The Search Bulletin (6 or 21 issues) $97.00/$300.00 _____

SUBTOTAL   _____

Virginia residents add 4½% sales tax   _____

POSTAGE/HANDLING ($3.00 for first
title and 75¢ for each additional book) $3.00

Number of additional titles x 75¢ ------------   _____

TOTAL ENCLOSED ----------------- _____

SHIP TO:

NAME _____

ADDRESS _____

_____

_____

[ ] I enclose check/moneyorder for $ _____ made
       payable to IMPACT PUBLICATIONS.

[ ] Please charge $ _____ to my credit card:

       Card # _____

       Expiration date: _____/_____

       Signature _____

UNIQUE JOB SEARCH SERVICES

JOB BANK USA ENROLLMENT

Enroll in JOB BANK USA's computerized electronic resume and job referral data base for a full year at the special price of only $30.00! Your association with the nation's premier employment data base company entitles you to receive these unique services:

- A personalized version of JOB BANK USA's unique electronic resume based on your work history and employment credentials;
- Storage of your electronic resume on the JOB BANK USA computer for one full year;
- Access to a toll free telephone number to make reasonable updates and corrections to your electronic resume;
- Exclusive discounts on a wide range of career management and job search services, books, and other resources;
- Unlimited referral to JOB BANK USA clients with open positions for which you are qualified; and
- *CAREERplus*, JOB BANK USA's quarterly newsletter published exclusively for data base enrollees.

To enroll, send $30.00 for the *Job Bank USA Enrollment* to: IMPACT PUBLICATIONS, 9104-N Manassas Dr., Manassas, VA 22111, Tel. 703/361-7300 or Fax 703/335-9486 (Visa or MasterCard).

THE SEARCH BULLETIN

If you're seeking an executive-level position in the $50,000-$250,000+ range, or just surveying today's job market, you should subscribe to *The Search Bulletin*. This nationwide publication provides access to hundreds of domestic and international job leads, networking opportunities, consulting and interim management assignments, job search resources, entrepreneurial alternatives, job hunting tips, and much more. Published twice monthly, this 25-30 page newsletter lists 160-200 new jobs each month in the fields of general management, marketing and sales, finance and accounting, and consulting/corporate planning. Most listings have not been advertised elsewhere. Your subscription also includes a completely confidential membership in the contract/networking program. 6 issues $97; 21 issues $300. Send $97 or $300 for *The Search Bulletin* to: Impact Publications, 9104-N Manassas Drive, Manassas, VA 22111, Tel. 703/361-7300 or Fax 703/335-9486 (Visa or MasterCard).

"JOBS AND CAREERS FOR THE 1990s" CATALOG

To receive your free copy of *"Jobs and Careers For the 1990s,"* complete the following form or send your name and address to:

IMPACT PUBLICATIONS
ATTN: Free Catalog
9104-N Manassas Drive
Manassas Park, VA 22111

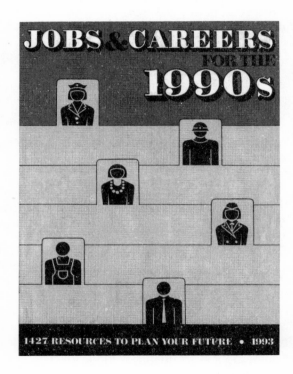

NAME _____

ADDRESS _____

_____

_____